BLACK BELT DIGITAL™

BLACK BELT DIGITAL™

GROW YOUR AESTHETICS BRAND, CLINIC OR MEDSPA BY BECOMING A BLACK BELT IN DIGITAL MARKETING

RICK O'NEILL, FRSA

DIGITAL CONSULTANT AND FOUNDER OF LTF

First paperback edition August 2023

Book design by Rick O'Neill, FRSA
Illustrations by Matthew Holland

978-1-80541-283-0 – Paperback
978-1-80541-284-7 – eBook
978-1-80541-285-4 – Hardback edition

www.rickoneill.co.uk
www.LTF.digital

CONTENTS

FOREWORD

Many of you reading this book will know me as the lead practitioner at Skinmed, Switzerland's most successful aesthetics brand.

And I do feel immensely lucky to have had the opportunities which have made Skinmed the renowned practice it is today. But the journey to Skinmed began almost 20 years ago, and I have never stopped learning, evolving, and taking advantage of new technologies in every part of my business.

Everyone in the profession will know that managing an aesthetics practice is hard. From the one-person practice to the global leader, there's no substitute for long hard hours and an obsession with patient centricity.

That means there's little room for error, and marketing is no different. In fact, smaller practices with smaller budgets have the most to lose and the least room for marketing mistakes.

In today's digital age, having a strong online presence is critical for businesses of all kinds, including aesthetic practices and clinics. From social media to search engine optimization, there are countless digital marketing strategies that can help you reach your target audience and grow your practice. However, navigating the world of digital marketing can be overwhelming, especially for those who are new to the field.

That's why I'm excited to introduce Rick O'Neill and his book, "The 'Black Belt' Guide to Digital Marketing for Aesthetic Clinics", full of actionable advice which every aesthetics business can follow, written exclusively for aesthetic practices and the professionals who work in them.

Rick is an industry icon and hugely experienced digital marketer who has worked for over 30 years with numerous aesthetic practices and clinics to help them achieve their marketing goals. In this book, he shares his wealth of knowledge and expertise, providing practical tips and strategies that you can use to take digital marketing to the next level.

Whether you're just starting out or looking to refine your existing digital marketing strategy, this book is an invaluable resource. Rick covers everything from website design and development to social media marketing, email marketing, and online advertising. He also provides insights into the unique challenges and opportunities that come with marketing for aesthetic practices, from unlocking the power of trust and authenticity to offering real-world examples and case studies to illustrate his points.

As you read this book, I encourage you to take notes, ask questions, and think critically about how you can apply these insights to your own aesthetic practice or clinic. Guided by Rick's expertise, you'll be well on your way to achieving your marketing goals, unlocking the keys to success and growing your practice in the digital age.

Felix J Bertram, Founder, Skinmed

DEDICATION

It's not easy being an entrepreneur, but it's even harder living with one! So, the biggest thanks go to my beautiful and inspiring wife, Saffron, and my children, Raife and Seren. In many ways, they inspire me, challenge me, support me, encourage me, and often bring me down to earth!

Thank you to my parents, Sam and Maria, without whom **none** of this would be possible, and to my brothers, Craig and Ashley, for their love and support.

Thank you also to the amazing team of people at my digital agency, LTF, who are talented, hard-working, and care deeply about the businesses and lives of all of our clients. Special thanks to Matt Holland for his dedication to LTF for over 15 years! Also to Simon Graham for his unwavering support over the last ten.

To all of my clients from the last 25 years, thank you for your faith in me and my team, and thank you for trusting part of your success to us.

Thank you to all of my friends and associates in the world of Medical Aesthetics from around the world who make this job fun, inspiring, and fascinating in equal measure.

Thank you to the incredible team at Merz Aesthetics, led by the indomitable Gillian Kennedy.

Thank you to Nick Saalfeld, without whom I could never have got this book over the line!

Thank you to Dr Tijion Esho, Dr Felix Bertram, Dr Sherina Balaratnum, Dr Sarah Tonks, Dr Ayad Harb, Dr Jake Sloane, David Segal, Dr Bob Khanna, and **so** many more with whom I have worked, presented, created and collaborated – and long may it all continue, as this is too much fun to stop now!

I dedicate this book to the memory of Simon Ayriss, or "Poppy" as he was known to us. He was an absolute force of positivity and brought our family together in ways we did not appreciate fully until he was gone. Thank you for teaching me to dream and to reach, and for the love you showed Saffron, Raife and Seren.

INTRODUCTION

Hello, I am Rick O'Neill, FRSA, a digital consultant to the medical aesthetics, cosmetic surgery, and pharmaceutical sectors.

With over 24 years of digital marketing expertise and 14 years as a specialist to the aesthetic sector I have produced numerous successful digital marketing and social media campaigns for private practices, high-profile surgeons and market-leading aesthetics brands.

I am Digital Consultant for Merz Aesthetics as well as the founder and MD of the award-winning Silverstone-based digital agency, LTF.

Welcome to the Digital Dojo!

Now I know what you're thinking...what is it with all this black belt stuff? Well, whilst a lot of people in aesthetics know me for being "that Digital marketing bloke", I am also a black belt and instructor in Taekwondo. I started out ten years ago by taking my then four-year-old son to the junior Taekwondo class. After being persuaded to get off the bench and join in, ten years later, my son has long since quit. But I stuck at it and I am now a first Dan black belt. I've competed nationally, and I was British Champion in the Taekwondo Power Test in 2019, taking home silver in Sparring the same year. It's something I'm passionate about, not just as a hobby but as a way of life.

I am also qualified to be a black belt in Digital Marketing. Having worked in the sector for 24 years now and built two successful digital agencies, I've learned what it takes to get real results from digital marketing. And with 14 years in cosmetic surgery and aesthetics, I've looked after marketing for numerous household-name brands and hundreds of clinics.

What brings Taekwondo and digital marketing together? In Taekwondo, we live by a series of tenets. We have to enact them consistently over almost a decade in order to achieve black-belt level. And I've learned over the years that a lot of the principles of a black belt apply to the creation of a digital marketing strategy too; at least, certainly if you want real and sustainable results.

It's about having a focused plan – who exactly are you trying to reach, where are they and for specifically what conditions or treatments?

You need to consistently show up. You can't get a black belt by turning up to just one Taekwondo class! Digital marketing is also not something you do once: it's a way of life, just like being a black belt.

It's also about being flexible in your approach, having the ability to think and act with speed, and having a power to your messaging and your digital platforms that stands you apart from the competition. You need to be able to adapt to the changing landscape of digital – platforms come and go and what worked last year, may not work next year.

And just like a fighter, you'll want to be efficient. In the dojo, energy is at a premium. In business, it's time and money which need to be conserved. You'll want to be efficient with your effort and investment into digital marketing – especially as I have never met an aesthetician who wasn't time-poor!

And finally, like every fight, it's a competition. Ultimately, it's about your digital presence being better than your nearest competitor's.

A changing world needs a black belt strategy

In this book, I will walk you through my Black Belt Content Strategy. It's a methodology which will ensure that your website, blogs, social content, Google posts, and ultimately you as the practitioner, become the go-to source for answers and services in your local area. We'll talk all things Google, from advertising to optimisation of your clinic's presence in Google Local Search results. And we'll cover social media from TikTok to Instagram.

But this is not just a guide based on completeness and best practice. It comes from a place of understanding that nothing in business stays the same – and marketing is faster-moving than most aspects of business. There are five big themes any marketer in aesthetics should be aware of today:

1. **The Importance of Content:** In order to attract new patients, you have to be an authority on the topics of skincare and medical aesthetics. Your potential patients are looking for answers to meaningful questions, and if *your* content isn't there to answer them, then your competitors' will. And by content, I mean more than an Instagram post: I mean articles, guides, emails, videos and more, on your website, on other social platforms, and on other relevant blog sites.

2. **Changing Search Behaviours:** In years gone by, the way people used Google was not very sophisticated. They used single-keyword searches and relied on traditional result listings. Today, we are much more sophisticated and knowledgeable both about how Google works and about aesthetics treatments. Potential patients will type in, or speak into a voice app, an entire comprehensive question about a skin condition or treatment type – and expect to find an answer. Not only that, but they'll go to local (Map Results) pages on Google once they've decided to take action – so you need to be there every time.

3. **Patients' Digital Expectations:** Look around you…Amazon Prime, iPhone Apps, Netflix, Uber, Deliveroo – everything is **super** slick, **super** convenient, and all of it is happening digitally. This means that our expectations of other digital touch points – for example, your clinic's website or booking system – are higher than ever. You must invest

to ensure that you are providing a seamless experience, optimised for mobile phones.

4. **Social Media Algorithms:** My team has found that the ability to reach and engage your existing or potential patients on Instagram is declining rapidly year-on-year. Thousands of new clinics join Instagram every year, and Instagram, therefore, prioritises paid posts – because they have shareholders to impress. If you just use Instagram, especially on a non-paid basis, you're probably shouting into the wind.

5. **Scaling with Automation:** And lastly, in order to scale an aesthetic clinic these days, you'll need more than a paper diary and a mobile. Automation of onboarding, reminders, and sophisticated workflows that bring patients back via highly personalised, timely messages…these are all business drivers, and we'll look at them here too.

THE HARD FACTS . . .

And it's an arms race. Some competitors will be working hard on their digital marketing and providing ever more sophisticated digital experiences. This means that if you want to get your fair share of the market, you have to raise your game too.

In 2022, I created The Digital Academy, in partnership with Merz Aesthetics. Well over 100 clinics have taken the 12-week program; and along the way, we have collected a lot of data (89 datapoints on each clinic, to be precise, adding up to nearly 9000 datapoints so far), so we know that a large percentage of clinics are lacking the modern marketing strategies required to compete in today's crowded market:

- 40% of clinics were getting less than 100 monthly views on their Google Profile
- 46% did not respond to patient reviews online
- 40% did not have a blog section on their websites

- 39% did not have a web booking system
- 61% did not include video content on their website
- 83% are apparently too shy to 'go live' on video themselves
- 47% weren't even using "before and after" on their website

UNDERSTANDING THE PATIENT JOURNEY

In this book, we'll take a deep dive into almost every aspect of aesthetics marketing. But it would be a mistake to pick and choose your campaign strategies according to what you fancy, or what seems fun. This is doomed to failure – and can be expensive.

You should always approach marketing through the lens of the customer. This is a mantra my agency team uses constantly; we should always be thinking, "What does the customer want?", and "What would they do?". Your marketing should therefore be constructed not via *your* journey, but via the patient's journey.

In my eyes, the first step of the patient's journey happens in their own mind when they look in the mirror or see themselves on a conference call. This is when the recognition of a problem or desire to change something about their appearance first occurs.

From that point forwards, 80% of their journey happens digitally. First, they research possible treatments or solutions to their perceived problem, likely on Google and on social media. They then start to seek validation and further insights from friends or peers – perhaps those who have already had the same type of treatment. This either happens in real life, or again on social media, forums, Reddit and innumerable other digital channels. Only once they've satisfied themselves with their research will they make a commitment to act; this is usually ultimately based on emotion backed up by the logic of their research.

At last, they then select a practitioner to book with. In more than 90% of cases, this takes place via a website or social channel and so the experience here can make the difference between a client going through with a transaction, abandoning the idea completely or going to another provider.

Then will they have their consultation, which, as you well know, is key in educating, reassuring and preparing them. But after that? Onboarding, care and follow-ups, etc. should be 90% digital too!

And when we map the digital elements of that patient journey that I've just walked you through, we get the critical building blocks required for any successful black belt digital strategy.

1. You need black-belt-grade content that attracts, educates and converts.
2. You need a black belt website, designed to educate, convert and onboard patients seamlessly, and in particular that provides a fantastic mobile experience. Over 85% of all web traffic to aesthetic clinics happens on a smartphone.
3. You need a strong presence on Google, specifically Google Local.
4. You need to be omnipresent on Social Channels so that when your potential patients are researching you and your work, they can find you on their favourite platform and see current and relevant content to help inform their decisions.
5. You need to have cutting-edge tools in place for email marketing and SMS so that you can communicate with patients in real time. Add to that a modern, clean, flexible CRM system that allows you to build sophisticated automation and workflows to re-engage and retain patients on an ongoing basis.

And that's the structure of this book.

LET'S GET STARTED!

I've written this book to be your go-to guide for navigating the ever-changing landscape of marketing for the aesthetics industry. My aim is to help you, the clinic owner, market your business more effectively by demystifying the latest trends. I've worked in aesthetics marketing for almost two decades, so I understand the business and your passion for helping other people look and feel their best.

Most aesthetics practice owners start their ventures because they're good at something quite specific: the treatment bit of the job! Very few want to become accountants, marketers or anything else at the back end of the business. And that's a problem: digital marketing has become indispensable in today's fast-paced, interconnected world, and the aesthetics industry is no exception. With potential clients searching for services online more than ever before, it is crucial that your clinic stands out in the digital realm. Investing time and resources into a robust online presence can help you reach more people, build trust and credibility, and ultimately, increase your client base.

You're going to need a modern, effective, user-friendly website that accurately showcases your brand and the services you offer. Your website is often the first point of contact between you and potential clients, so it's essential that it makes a great first impression. In addition to providing information about your treatments, your website can also serve as a platform to share client testimonials, before and after photos, and educational content, all of which can help to attract and retain clients. We'll look at all these issues here.

Social media is another crucial element of digital marketing. Platforms like Instagram, Facebook, and TikTok have become powerful tools for aesthetics practitioners, helping them to engage with potential clients and showcase their work. By sharing compelling visuals, how-tos and behind-the-scenes glimpses into your clinic, you can connect with your audience on a more personal level and foster that all-important sense of trust and credibility.

This stuff matters because we're in the middle of an arms race. While the aesthetics industry is booming, it's highly competitive. With new clinics opening up all the time (and not all of them are particularly high quality), it can be difficult to differentiate yourself from the competition and make your clinic stand out. This book will offer strategies to help you develop a unique selling proposition that will set you apart and resonate with your target audience.

Most aesthetics clinic owners struggle to find the time and resources to dedicate to marketing efforts. If you're a solo practitioner, I'll bet good money you're reading this late into the night. Running a clinic is no mean feat, and it's easy for marketing initiatives to take a back seat to day-to-day operations. I hope that here I'll help you to avoid mistakes, efficiently allocate your time and resources to marketing tasks, and automate some processes so that your marketing efforts are consistent and effective without constant supervision.

It's also essential to be aware of the latest marketing trends and adapt your strategies accordingly. By embracing new approaches and technologies, you can better engage with your audience, attract new clients and foster loyalty among your existing clientele. Here are just a few of the ways marketing is developing which are particularly relevant to aesthetics professionals:

- **Personalisation:** Today's clients expect personalised experiences, tailored to their unique needs and preferences. By using data-driven insights and segmenting your audience, you can create targeted marketing campaigns that resonate with potential clients on a deeper level. This doesn't have to be complicated – think customised email campaigns or tailored social media content.

- **Influencer Marketing:** Few businesses are more image-conscious than aesthetics, and that means it's ideal for influencer marketing. Collaborating with influencers has become a popular and effective way to increase a clinic's visibility and reach a wider audience. Partnering with the right influencers, who share your values and have an engaged following (especially!), can help you build credibility with potential clients.

- **Going all in on Video**: Video has emerged as a dominant form of content, with platforms like YouTube, TikTok, and Instagram Reels playing a significant role in shaping consumer behaviour. Incorporating video into your marketing strategy can help you showcase your treatments, share client testimonials, and engage with your audience in a more immersive and authentic way. But video can also be expensive, so we'll focus on the ways it really drives value.

- **Reputation Management:** In the aesthetics industry, your reputation is everything. Online reviews and word-of-mouth referrals can make or break your clinic. It's crucial to monitor and manage your online reputation by responding to reviews, addressing concerns, and actively seeking out feedback from clients. I also really like reviews because they're highly localised – you're reaching people in your local area; people who absolutely are your next customers-in-waiting.

As we embark on this journey together, let me make it clear: you don't have to do everything you find here, and you don't have to fill every gap. I'm going to give you the knowledge, tools, and confidence to effectively market your aesthetics clinic but if you use even 25% of these techniques, you'll be doing just fine. By understanding the importance of digital marketing, tackling the unique challenges of aesthetics clinic marketing, and staying informed about current trends, you'll be well-positioned to grow your business. So, let's get cracking on a black-belt ninja approach to bringing in new money!

DEFINING YOUR TARGET AUDIENCE: DO YOUR RESEARCH!

DEMOGRAPHICS

You'd probably be happy to have anyone come through your door. And that's fine. But there is such a thing as an ideal customer. Understanding the demographics of your target audience is crucial in tailoring marketing strategies for aesthetic practices. It will enable you to identify your ideal client and create marketing campaigns that resonate with them. Here are some of the key demographic factors to consider:

- **Age:** Age is a significant determinant in the demand for aesthetic treatments. Different age groups have varying concerns, and your marketing messages should address those concerns accordingly. For instance, younger clients may be more interested in beauty treatments and preventative care, while older clients may seek solutions for wrinkles and age spots.
- **Gender:** Both men and women are potential clients for aesthetic practices (demand from men is increasing dramatically!) but they will have different preferences and concerns. Ensure that your marketing materials and services cater to both audiences, or those you intend to target most.
- **Location:** Geographic location must influence your target audience, as clients' preferences and aesthetic concerns may vary based on regional tastes, and more importantly, how easy it is to get to your

practice. Ultra-high-end practices will attract customers from further afield (so will practices blessed with being in well-connected cities), whereas if you're in a more local catchment, you should be looking to get more clients from just around the corner.

- **Income:** Aesthetic treatments can be seen as luxury services. Understanding the income levels of your target audience and the local area will help you price your services accordingly and develop marketing campaigns that appeal to clients' budgets. Beware selling on price though – in aesthetics, talking price too often will make you look cheap – and that's not a good look!
- **Occupation:** Your clients' occupations may dictate their aesthetic concerns and preferences. Professionals who work in industries that place a premium on appearance, such as media or fashion, may be particularly focused on the sort of services you offer.
- **Family Status:** Finally, family status, such as being a parent or having a partner, can influence an individual's priorities and willingness to invest in aesthetic treatments. Are you targeting "yummy mummies of a certain age" in a well-off area, or younger people with plenty of personal disposable income who don't have children to spend their money on?

After analyzing these demographic factors, you'll be in a good place to profile your ideal client. Keeping them in mind will help you create targeted marketing campaigns that speak directly to their needs, preferences, and beauty ambitions.

PERSONAS

If you need to paint a picture of this ideal client while you're thinking through your marketing plan, you'll need what's called a "buyer persona". A buyer persona is a realistic but fictional representation of your ideal client, preferably based on real data and market research.

Creating buyer personas allows you to:

- **Personalize your marketing messages:** By understanding your target audience's motivations, desires, and needs, you can create marketing materials that resonate with them on a personal level.
- **Prioritize marketing effort and spend:** Knowing which personas are most valuable to your business helps you allocate resources and focus on the marketing initiatives that will yield the best results.
- **Develop better products and services:** Buyer personas provide insights into your clients' needs, helping you design treatments and packages that cater specifically to their requirements.

Personas provide valuable insights that you can use to convey your message to the right audience at the right time. They also enable you to perform market research, targeted advertising, usability testing, and keyword research more efficiently.

THE DIGITAL MARKETING INSTITUTE

To build your buyer personas, start with the demographic data we discussed above. Then, identify their motivations and needs: What services do they want? What moves them to think about beauty, aesthetics and wellbeing? Consider their primary motivations, such as self-improvement, confidence boosting, or addressing specific aesthetic concerns. Equally important are their pain points, which may include dissatisfaction with their appearance, previous negative experiences with aesthetics treatments, or concerns about the cost and safety of treatments (especially if they've had a bad experience elsewhere).

That brings us to understanding their goals and values: What might drive their decision-making process? Are they looking for long-lasting results, minimal downtime so that they can get back to work, or a more natural look? Do they prioritize safety, quality, and your professional expertise? Understanding these motivations will help you tailor your messaging and services accordingly.

There are more useful questions to ask, based less on your customer's needs and more on the way they like to buy.

Explore their sources of information. Where do they get their information about aesthetics treatments and practitioners from? Are they more likely to rely on recommendations from friends and family, online reviews, or social media influencers? Knowing their preferred sources of information can guide your marketing efforts and make sure you don't waste money on efforts that don't work!

Look at your clients' personalities, values, attitudes, interests, and life-styles, because there may be mileage in appealing to these. For instance, you may identify a segment of clients who prioritize eco-friendly and ethically sourced products or another segment that values luxury and exclusivity. By considering these factors, you can better tailor your market-ing message to resonate with each group.

And then have a think about what marketers call the "purchasing jour-ney". We usually don't just find the nearest supplier and buy on a whim. Map out the typical steps your clients take before deciding on an aes-thetics treatment or provider. This will likely include doing some initial research, comparing different clinics, treatments and prices, schedul-ing consultations, and making a final purchase decision. You'll want to have marketing that works for each of these stages (including doing a great initial consultation yourself). Similarly, you may already have some knowledge of how clients today behave and interact with your services. How often do they visit? What are their preferred treatments? Do they respond to promotions? By understanding your clients' behaviours, you can offer targeted incentives that encourage repeat visits and build customer loyalty.

Once you have asked these questions (it's okay if you don't have a perfect answer – having a bit of insight will be fine!), it's time to bring your personas to life. Even if it's just a brief bullet-point picture, give each persona a name, create some facts about them, and get to the stage where you feel like you really know them well.

For example, if one of your personas is a 35-year-old woman – Sarah, an office worker – who has never had an aesthetic treatment before, values natural-looking results and is looking for a bit of a boost, but is concerned about the safety of treatments, you'll decide that your marketing materials should emphasize the safety measures taken at your clinic and showcase before-and-after photos that highlight natural outcomes. Similarly, if another persona is a 50-year-old man – Keith, an HR Director – interested in treatments to combat the signs of ageing, your messaging should focus on the efficacy of your treatments in addressing age-related concerns and the simplicity of your treatments.

Two more points on personas.

First, we've written them in the plural. You may well have more than one persona. Don't target ten, since you're bound to mess it up but do recognise that there may be two or even three types of clients who are right in your sweet spot.

Second, remember also that buyer personas aren't static – they should be updated regularly as you gather new information about your customers (especially any feedback you receive) or as market trends shift. Review and refine them every six months or so.

MARKET RESEARCH

Now, if you're not a giant business with a big marketing department (and you probably wouldn't be reading this if you were), everything we've done in this chapter so far will have come from your head, with a bit of thinking over a cup of tea (or something stronger) at the end of a hard day.

If you get the chance, it's worth spending a bit of time validating that thinking with market research; or put more simply, simple conversations with real people. Don't, under any circumstances, do market research with your friends or family. They won't be honest. You need to talk to real customers, or better still, real people in your local area who aren't customers but who are close enough to your personas that they should be.

Here are some options:

- **Surveys and Questionnaires:** Surveys and questionnaires are popular tools for collecting data from a large number of respondents. They can be distributed online, through email or social media (which makes it easy to reach lots of new people), or even in person at your clinic or events. If you're not already getting feedback from your customers, you should be! To make your survey effective, ask clear, concise and simple questions, especially about their preferences and attitudes towards aesthetic treatments. The one problem with online surveys is that many people don't like giving personal information (like their income or family status) to an online form. It might be better to spend ten minutes with a client after a consultation, gently asking them for their opinion to help you build a better business.

- That brings us to more **In-Depth Interviews**, which offer a more personal perspective on your target customer's needs and preferences. These one-on-one conversations allow you to explore complex topics and gather detailed insights that won't be possible in a group setting or online survey. Now that we're all comfortable on Zoom, you can easily conduct these interviews via video call, too.

- Finally, you might consider **Focus Groups**, small, moderated discussions that involve a group of individuals who represent your typical customers. These allow you to dive deeper into your clients' thoughts, feelings, and motivations, providing rounded, conversational insight. Organize focus groups to discuss various topics, such as the appeal of specific treatments, reactions to marketing materials, or the factors that drive client loyalty. The great thing about focus groups is that once one participant starts talking, others will almost certainly open up. It's a great way to get honest answers! The bad thing about focus groups is that getting four people together in the same place at the same time can be a nightmare. Do it informally, on a Monday evening, in the local pub or coffee shop.

There is another sort of market research – the sort you buy off-the-shelf. Industry reports, market analyses, and competitor information can be horribly expensive, but you'll be amazed how much information is available free of charge from your local library or council offices. What are the local regeneration plans? How is transport changing in your area? These sorts of sources can provide valuable insights into the overall market size, potential opportunities and any trends (good or bad) to be aware of. This secondary research can also, crucially, help you benchmark your business against competitors and identify any areas for improvement.

Once you've got a bundle of information – or at least a few conversations under your belt, it's time to analyze and use the results. There's really only one golden nugget here: looking for patterns and recurring themes. Common client challenges, pain points and preferences are what we're looking for: these are the reliable triggers which will inform your marketing strategies.

You should now have some confidence in your customers. If you don't, go back and do some more thinking! And if the people who seem to be willing to use your business aren't actually the sort of people you thought your business was catering to, then it's time for a rethink. The customer is always right, and if you want to earn money rather than pour it away, you'll need to face some home truths and refine your offer to attract the people who are actually willing to pay.

With customers dealt with, there's one more research aspect to consider: your competitors!

Conducting a thorough competitive analysis will help you identify your competitors, pinpoint their strengths and weaknesses, and refine your offer to differentiate your practice.

You have three fundamental competitors:

- **Direct competitors:** Businesses that offer similar services in the same geographic area.
- **Indirect competitors:** Alternative or complementary services that can potentially fulfil the same customer needs. There will, for example, be beauty professionals who might not conduct aesthetics procedures, but who are nevertheless part of your market.
- **Doing nothing:** Don't forget; other than utilities like water and electricity, most of us also have the option of not buying anything at all.

To identify your competitors, run online searches for practices within your service area. Make use of search engines, social media platforms, and local business directories. You might also attend industry events, but what matters is seeing the competition through the eyes of the customer: Who comes up on the first page of Google? Who is advertising in the local area?

Once you've identified relevant competitors, collect information on their services, pricing and the audiences they are targeting. It's easy to find a thumb-in-the-air idea of these from their websites, social media channels, customer reviews, and promotional materials. Make sure you understand:

- The services they offer and corresponding prices
- Promotional strategies and the channels they use
- Brand positioning – are they luxury, every-day, local, price-conscious...?
- Any customer reviews and testimonials
- Any selling points they particularly promote, or competitive advantages – especially ones you feel might be challenging to compete with!

And then it's a simple case of assessing the strengths and weaknesses of each competitor and applying them to your own practice. What sets them apart? What attracts clients to their practice, and where might they equally be lacking in their service offerings or marketing efforts? On that basis, what traits do you want to replicate, because they're good practice and will attract a profitable clientele? And what traits do you want to avoid, because you need to find a niche that's right for you? The goal here is to uncover opportunities for your practice to stand out and provide a superior experience.

CHECKLIST

☑ Identify your demographic target and the factors which influence them.

☑ Create buyer personas using demographic data, motivations, needs, and pain points.

☑ Understand your ideal clients' health and aesthetic goals and values.

☑ Explore your clients' sources of information and their marketing preferences.

☑ Consider the purchasing journey and client behaviour.

☑ Conduct market research (Surveys, interviews, etc.)

☑ Conduct a competitive analysis: collect information on competitors' services, pricing, and target audience and differentiate your practice from competitors.

☑ Develop targeted marketing campaigns based on your ideal client profiles.

☑ Revisit: continuously review and update your understanding of your audience and competitors and adjust your marketing strategies accordingly.

YOUR WEBSITE – THE FOUNDATION OF AN ONLINE PRESENCE

BRAND AND IDENTITY

Your website is the front door to almost everything you do online, so that's going to be the focus of this chapter.

That's not 100% true today – there are quite a few practitioners who use social sites like Instagram as their first port of call, but your website is still likely to be the engine room of your digital activities. Not only that, you Insta fan, putting all your eggs in the social media basket is a major risk. You do not own your social media accounts, and they can easily be taken from you at any moment. Your website, conversely, is all yours. Furthermore, according to a study by TechNewsWorld.com, social media account takeovers (that's hacks to you and me) have risen over 1000% since 2020.

So investing in the website that you own and control isn't just good business; it's a critical risk mitigation strategy.

But either way, hold your horses. I know that after all the research in the previous chapter, you're desperate to get out there and build your marketing, but we need to do a bit of planning first.

We're not looking at your customers. Or your competitors. It's time to talk about you.

As an aesthetics practice manager, you know the importance of appearances better than most! Your clients come to you for treatments that enhance their looks, and your brand needs an attractive, compelling identity, too. The process of crafting your brand message and identity is essential in building a strong and enduring online presence. Here's how to do it:

- **Define Your Core Values:** These are the principles that guide your business and set you apart from the competition. Ask what is truly important to you as a practice and what you want to communicate to your clients. What's going to make you shine? You might like some of these:

  - ☐ A commitment to client satisfaction
  - ☐ Prioritizing safety and professional standards – your qualifications
  - ☐ Offering innovative, cutting-edge evidence-based treatments
  - ☐ Promoting body positivity and self-confidence
  - ☐ A sense of luxury and no-compromise service

  Whatever your ambition, these core values should be authentic and reflect the passion and drive behind your practice. They should also resonate with your target audience – the people we so carefully worked out in the last chapter. If your values, the things you stand for and which motivate you to get out of bed every morning, don't match up with this audience, then that's a red flag you should resolve before proceeding.
- **Discover Your Unique Selling Proposition (USP):** In a crowded market, it's important to differentiate yourself from competitors. Your Unique Selling Proposition (USP) should succinctly communicate what makes your aesthetics practice unique and appealingly different to the rest. Think about the specific strengths and offerings of your practice that set you apart. Perhaps you specialize in a particular treatment, or your clinic boasts a world-renowned practitioner. Whatever your USP, it belongs at the heart of your brand message and identity.

11

- **Create a Consistent Visual Identity:** Your visual identity is a critical component of your brand. It includes your logo, colour palette, typography, and any other visual elements that represent your practice. Consistent branding helps create a recognizable, memorable image for your clients. When designing your visual identity, consider the emotions and values you want to convey. For example, a modern, minimalistic design might represent professionalism and cutting-edge treatments, while a more classic, elegant look could evoke luxury and prestige. Either way, a good place to start is to run a quick web search for other practices or similar businesses and work out what you like and what you don't. If you're talking to an agency to get your website built, they won't particularly need to know why you like or don't like certain styles – just knowing your preferences will do just fine.

- **Craft Your Brand Voice:** If your brand identity is the visual aspect of your company's personality, then your brand voice is the tone and style of your written and spoken communications. It should reflect your core values and speak naturally to your audience. A consistent brand voice will help to establish trust and familiarity with your clients. When crafting your brand voice, think about the personality you want your practice to embody. Are you friendly and approachable, or more formal and sophisticated? Consider your target audience and their preferences when developing your brand voice. For example, if your target clientele consists of younger clients, a casual, relatable tone might be more effective than something more formal. If you have any doubts about this, simply go with writing in a human, conversational style. Like this book. There are, of course, exceptions. When writing about invasive treatments, for example, readers will want clarity, reliability and trust; so the more conversational approach won't work.

- **Create a Brand Story:** Have you ever wondered why everyone appearing on the X-Factor or any other game show has a story? It's all part of our brands – as businesses or as people. A compelling brand story can help connect with clients on an emotional level, making your practice more relatable, memorable, and – crucially – different from the next one in line. Your brand story should communicate your practice's mission, history, and unique qualities in a way that reso-nates with your target audience. It should answer questions like: Why did you start your aesthetics practice? How have you made a differ-ence in your clients' lives? Show that you're not in the business just to make money (although that's not a bad thing) but because you're motivated by making a difference.

Consistency is key when it comes to your brand identity. Ensure that your brand message, visual identity, and brand voice are consistently repre-sented across all your online channels, including your website, social media profiles, and email marketing campaigns. This helps create a cohesive brand experience for your clients, making your practice easily recognizable and memorable.

THE EIGHT BIG WEBSITE SUCCESS FACTORS

I appreciate we've taken a bit of a detour into brand strategy there, but now we're in good shape to actually put together a website. I think there are eight key website success factors – we'll look at all of them in various degrees of detail in the rest of this book.

- **Search Engine Optimisation (SEO):** The biggest priority is for cus-tomers to find your website in the first place, so it's vital that your website is built and optimised for Search engines like Google. The fastest way to ensure this is to have a site built on the WordPress platform, which is known to be favoured by Google, and to have an SEO professional or web developer with SEO experience work on the site's metadata and structure to make it easy for Google to find and navigate it. Whatever system you use (SquareSpace, for example, is pretty good), SEO is crucial, and we'll look at optimising your content in a later section.

■ **Blog:** Your website needs a blog. This is where all your articles that answer key patient questions will live. This is what will bring in additional, highly relevant traffic to your clinic's website. It's also material that you can then repurpose into Social posts, Google posts, and email campaigns. We cover all of these elsewhere in this book, so get yourself a blog page!

■ **Design:** Your website is where patients form a significant part of their impression of you and your clinic. If your website looks as though it was banged out on a Friday night, you'll reap the rewards of that poverty of thinking. The statistics tell us that website visitors decide whether they want to stay on a site in less than 50 milliseconds! That means that in the initial few moments, style is dramatically more important than substance. And if you don't think that's the case, you probably shouldn't be an aesthetics professional…

■ **Mobile:** With around 85% of aesthetics website traffic today happening on a mobile, your website needs to work fast and navigate easily on the small screen.

■ **Speed:** By which I mean the speed at which your website loads up. We're increasingly intolerant of hanging around, and if your website takes too long to load (even by moments), customers will go elsewhere. Interestingly, Google is just as intolerant. In 2022, Google introduced the Core Web Vitals test, which determines whether, in Google's view, your website is fast enough to load and easy enough to use, both on a laptop and mobile devices. Many websites today fail this test, but those that pass it get the lion's share of traffic – because Google deems them to be worthier of higher positions in search results. Annoyingly, it's not always easy to spot a slow-loading website – if you've got great wi-fi, you might never notice! Try loading your website in a few different places, including on a phone in a place with fairly dodgy reception. To improve your site's load time, consider the following strategies (this is technical stuff, so get help if you need it!):

☐ Compress images and videos: Use tools like TinyPNG or Compressor.io to compress files without sacrificing quality.

☐ Use browser caching: Browser caching stores a version of your website on a user's device, allowing it to load more quickly during future visits. Many web builder platforms and content management systems offer caching plugins that can help improve load times.

☐ Minimize the use of large or complex scripts: Excessive JavaScript, CSS, or other code can slow down your site. Keep your website's code clean and well-organized and consider using minification tools to further improve performance.

■ **Structure.** Patients don't think the same way as you do. They will think of their problems first, not a service, the name of a device or a treatment modality. Therefore, as well as having services or treatments listed, consider guiding patients with a focus on their conditions or the emotional outcomes they want to achieve. "I want to look younger" or "I want to age well" can be dramatically more effective than "Fillers".

■ **Guidance.** A structure which meets your prospective patients' emotional needs is only the start of your engagement process. A first-time visitor to your website may be looking at aesthetics for the first time too, and they may need encouragement and assistance. Use content to offer clear and reliable guidance – including pictures and video which give greater reassurance. You might also consider the next generation of chatbots and AI assistants to maintain a dialogue and build rapport.

■ **Lead Magnets.** The final essential in producing your website sounds like a bit of marketing-speak, but it's not that complex. Most aesthetics websites offer two fundamental outcomes: book a service or leave. There's a crucial third option. We can offer educational content in exchange for an email address. That educational content could be a guide to a particular condition, an educational video series on skin-care routines, or a treatment walkthrough. Either way, it's content that has enough relevance and value for an interested visitor to take the small step of surrendering their email address to gain access to it. We can then, with their consent, send them a series of automated follow-up emails (or other experiences) to nurture them back towards a consultation. It's a Marketing 101 principle, but it's one which is often forgotten. And in aesthetics, where everyone will need multiple touchpoints before they have the confidence to make a purchase decision, lead magnets should be front-and-centre of your approach.

BUILDING YOUR WEBSITE

If you've **already got a website**, you can jump forward a little.

If you're **thinking of commissioning an agency or web designer**, please read the following (you'll find more on commissioning an agency in the final chapter):

- Professional web designers are in high demand. If you are cold-called or spammed, run a mile. Get a recommendation from someone you know.
- If a website is offered to you for free, run even further. At best, it will give your customers a sub-optimal experience which will cost your business far more than a good website. At worst, it will tie you in to systems that don't meet your needs or even painful unexpected costs. Not only that, but on a freebie, you will have no recourse for reworks, changes, turn-around times, etc. Lastly, let me ask you – would you let me inject you for free? Does that fill you with confidence? Exactly. Customer conversion online is intensely competitive, and you deserve

better than a second-rate website which haemorrhages value. I use a checklist of over 300 elements to ensure a website is up to scratch.

■ If a web designer is using one of the many platform systems to build your website (WIX, GoDaddy, 123, IONOS), then they are not a web designer. They are marketing consultants at best, who happen to have added web design to their list of services. Professional web designers use professional tools, such as WordPress, ExpressionEngine and Drupal. Indeed, if you choose to build your own website (see below), we recommend WordPress. If it's good enough – and flexible enough – for you to do on your own, you really don't need to use a platform.

■ Finally, don't ever be bullied. Ask questions. And if you feel like the person in a car repair garage who is being slowly beaten around the head with jargon, then again, walk away. Before you enter into any web design agreement, you have a right to be sure that you are getting what you need. Make sure that you both have the same expectations. A "website" can mean anything from a single page up to a 1000-page site with booking systems, blogs, diaries, e-commerce, etc. Professional websites can range from £4000 up to £50,000 depending on the specification. Ask how the web designer intends to handle SEO, how maintenance will work, how they will ensure a good mobile experience, and who will own the website if you decide to part company.

If you're **taking your first steps to building your own website** (or if you're looking to change platforms), the following advice will be useful:

■ **Choosing a Domain Name:** Your domain name is the web address where your site can be found – www.susansmithaesthetics.co.uk or similar. It should be easy to remember, spell, and type. Ideally, it should include your business name, be relevant to your industry, and have a .co.uk or .com extension to reflect your UK-based practice. To register a domain, use a reputable domain registrar (e.g. GoDaddy,

123-Reg), and ensure your chosen domain is available and affordable. If a .co.uk or .com address is not available, most providers will automatically offer you an alternative, e.g. '.site' or '.london'. Obviously, that's not much use if you're in Berwick, but you get the idea.

- **Selecting a Web Builder:** There are numerous web-builder systems available to help you create a professional-looking website without the need for extensive coding knowledge. The most popular options are WordPress and SquareSpace. Each platform has its own set of features, templates, and pricing plans, and it's essential to do your research and choose the one that best suits your needs and budget. As I said above, I genuinely think that basic platforms like Wix are pretty grim. And we genuinely think that while WordPress is hard to get your head around, it's easily the most durable and will allow you to achieve the most for your business. WordPress powers around one-third of the internet, so it's not going to disappear anytime soon. And most creative agencies offer WordPress skills, so it'll be easy to grow the site when you get some help.

Whichever platform you use, just making your site "look nice" won't do! Your website should be easy to navigate, visually appealing, and designed to convert visitors into clients. To achieve this, consider the following design principles:

- **Clear and easy-to-use navigation:** Ensure your site has a simple menu that helps users quickly find the information they're looking for. Use clear headings and subheadings to guide visitors through your content.
- **Consistent branding:** Use consistent colours, fonts, and imagery across your website to create a brand experience you're proud of. In the world of aesthetics, image is everything!
- **Engaging visuals:** Use high-quality images, videos, and graphics to showcase your services and convey a professional image.

- **Tell customers what to do!:** This is called a "call to action" (or CTA): Encourage visitors to take specific actions, such as booking a consultation or signing up for your newsletter, by placing well-designed CTAs throughout your site.

With more people accessing websites via their mobile phones, we mentioned above that it's also crucial to ensure your website is "mobile-responsive". This means your site will automatically adapt to different screen sizes and function as smoothly on smartphones and tablets as it does on full-size PCs. Most web-builder platforms offer mobile-responsive templates, but it's worth testing your site on various devices to ensure a seamless user experience.

Ensuring that your website is accessible to all users with physical and mental disabilities and impairments isn't just best practice, good for business, and the right thing to do, but there are also elements of accessibility which are a legal requirement. To make your website more accessible, use clear and concise language – keep your content straightforward and easy to understand. Provide alternative text (also called "alt text") for images, which is descriptive text that ensures screen readers can convey the information in pictures to visually impaired users. Similarly, use descriptive text for links: instead of using a generic phrase like "click here," use meaningful link text that adequately describes the destination page.

For those with mobility issues, make sure users can navigate your site using only a keyboard, without the need for a mouse. And for those with visual impairments, choose colours with sufficient contrast to make your content easily readable. If that sounds like a lot of stuff to consider, don't worry. You can automatically test your site for accessibility using tools like WAVE or Google's Lighthouse. They'll give you a performance score and identify any areas for improvement.

We'll look at content again in more detail later when this book will deal in more depth with "content marketing", the ways in which we reach out to new clients. But the content you put on your website does, of course, matter. The good news is you don't need a lot of it! When did you last say to yourself, "Ooh, I wish there was more stuff for me to wade through"? Never. What matters is that what you do provide is informative, engaging and laser-focused on being relevant to your target audience and their needs at any one moment. Write clear and easily accessible (but short and simple) service descriptions which explain the aesthetics services you offer, along with their benefits. Showcase the results of your work with high-quality before-and-after images (make sure you have proper consent from clients before using these!). It's been proven time and again that before-and-after pictures are the most effective marketing tool in aesthetics. On top of that, be sure to include testimonials from satisfied clients to build trust with potential customers. If you get e.g. Google reviews, you can embed these automatically into your site.

And then there's your blog or resources section, which will offer helpful articles, guides, or resources related to your services, to help establish your expertise and credibility with customers and in the industry. Don't go crazy writing thousands of blogs – you don't have time for that! As we saw above, your blogs are there to do real work, bringing in search-delivered prospects. A few well-placed blogs covering themes which really matter to your audience will do nicely. More on that later.

Companies that blog have 434% more indexed pages (pages showing up on search engines like Google) than those that don't.

HTTPS://WWW.SMALLBIZGENIUS.NET/BY-THE-NUMBERS/SEO-STATISTICS/

Finally, don't forget your contact information. Make it easy for potential clients to get in touch with you by providing a phone number (yes – that totally still needs to be there), your email address, and your physical location.

OPTIMIZING YOUR WEBSITE FOR SEARCH ENGINES: THE DARK ART OF SEO!

Search Engine Optimization (SEO) is the skill of making your website more visible and accessible to search engines like Google and Bing, and therefore more attractive to potential customers. It's the equivalent of putting on perfume or after-shave – when you're more attractive, you get more interest! A well-optimized website can therefore help your aesthetics practice rank higher in search results, increasing your online visibility and attracting potential clients. In this section, we'll discuss the strategies and best practice for optimizing your website for search engines.

The thing is, there are hundreds of such strategies. And they change all the time – in fact, search engines constantly amend their ranking tools to provide better results. The way to look at SEO is it's incremental. You don't need to use every SEO technique to improve your website (you'll never get it all done, anyway), but every technique you do use will make an incremental contribution to your website's effectiveness.

Got that? Let's dive in – pick the ideas which work for you:

- **Keyword Research:** Keywords are the words and phrases that we enter into our search engine of choice when looking for information or services. Identifying the right keywords and including them in your content is crucial for driving relevant, high-quality traffic to your website. When researching the most popular and relevant keywords related to your aesthetics practice, Tools like Google Ads Keyword Planner, Moz Keyword Explorer and SEMrush can help you identify keyword opportunities. Focus on keywords that are relevant to your services, have a good search volume, and moderate competition (as Meatloaf said, two out of three ain't bad). Incorporate them strategically into your website content, including titles, headings, body text, and meta descriptions. Be careful not to overuse keywords, as "keyword stuffing" can result in search engines penalising you and deprioritising your material.

- **Create High-Quality, Relevant Content:** Creating engaging, informative content that addresses the interests and needs of your target audience is important for SEO success. Search engines prioritise websites that provide valuable content to users. Publish new content such as blog posts, articles, and case studies regularly if you can – this can help improve your search engine rankings and keep visitors engaged. When creating content, focus religiously on addressing common questions and concerns related to your services and highlighting the unique aspects of your aesthetics practice. Be sure to optimize the content you produce with those target keywords where you can, so long as you don't compromise readability and user satisfaction.

- **Think about Site Structure and Navigation:** A well-organized website with clear navigation makes it easier for search engines to index your content. Use descriptive, keyword-rich titles and headings for your pages to improve your website's visibility in search results. You should also create an XML sitemap – a file that lists all the pages on your website – (tools like Webflow will do this in seconds) and submit it to search engines like Google and Bing. This helps search engines understand the structure of your website and index your content more efficiently.

- **Build High-Quality Backlinks:** Backlinks are links to your site which come from other websites. They are an important signal for search engines in determining your website's credibility and authority. If lots of other sites link to your website, the search engines reason that you must be a more important and credible site than other less well-linked options. Building high-quality backlinks can therefore significantly improve your website's search engine rankings. To earn backlinks, focus on creating valuable, shareable content that other websites and influencers in aesthetics will want to link to. You can also engage in guest blogging, collaborate with industry partners and participate in relevant online communities to increase your website's exposure and attract backlinks. Remember, quality is more important than quantity when it comes to backlinks: focus on earning links from reputable, authoritative websites within your niche.

- **Use Social Media to Promote Your Content:** Although social media signals don't have a direct impact on search engine rankings, promoting your content on social media platforms can help drive traffic to your website and increase your content's visibility. Sharing your blog posts, articles, and other valuable content on platforms like Facebook, Instagram and Twitter can encourage users to visit your website and potentially link to your content, contributing to your overall SEO efforts.

You really can spend all day every day working on SEO. Cover off some of the above and your website will definitely be working at maximum performance. Be sure to come back and track your SEO performance every few months – as I said above, it's a moving feast. Use tools like Google Analytics and Google's Search Console to track metrics such as organic search traffic, click-through rates, bounce rates, and the average time spent on your website. Analyzing this data can help you understand which strategies are working well and where adjustments may be needed.

ADVANCED WEBSITE FUNCTIONALITY

The above website build advice and optimisation will comfortably get your practice off the ground. But an exceptional online experience will take things to the next level, also saving time and cutting your costs. Advanced website functionality can help streamline your practice's operations, enhance user experience, and ultimately contribute to the growth of your practice.

An **online booking system** should be first on your wish-list. It allows clients to book appointments directly through your website, making the process more convenient and efficient for both your clients and your team. Expect to offer:

- **24/7 appointment scheduling and changes:** Clients can book appointments at their convenience, even outside of operating hours.
- **Reduce no-shows:** Automated reminders and confirmations help minimize missed appointments, meaning your time is valued more highly
- **Streamline administrative tasks:** Online booking systems reduce the time your staff (or you!) spend on basic scheduling.

When selecting an online booking system, make sure it's easy to use. Check out customization options to ensure it meets your brand and visual standards. Also, check for integration with any existing practice management software – otherwise, you'll just be doubling up on effort and errors will creep in. Popular booking systems for aesthetics practices include Acuity Scheduling, Timely, and SimplyBook.me.

Integrating **social media** into your website is an effective way to connect with your audience, increase your online visibility, and showcase your practice's personality. Here are some ways to integrate social media into your website:

- **Social sharing buttons:** Make it easy for visitors to share your content on platforms like Facebook, Twitter, and Instagram by adding social sharing buttons to your blog posts, articles, and other valuable content.
- **Social media feeds:** Embed your practice's social media feeds directly on your website, showcasing your latest posts, promotions, and client testimonials. (This is super easy with WordPress).
- **Follow buttons:** Encourage website visitors to follow your social media profiles by adding follow buttons to your website's header, footer, or sidebar.

Integrating your **email marketing** platform with your website can help you grow your email list and streamline your marketing efforts. To do this, simply take every opportunity to get users to give you their email address, with two such opportunities by default:

1. Encourage website visitors to subscribe to an email newsletter by including sign-up forms in prominent places like the homepage or a blog sidebar.
2. Set up email automation sequences that trigger based on specific actions, such as booking an appointment, to keep clients engaged and informed.

Live chat and chatbot features can enhance your clients' experience by providing real-time support and assistance. By offering immediate responses to questions and concerns, you can improve customer satisfaction and increase the likelihood of booking appointments.

It's unlikely that you're resourced to provide live chat with clients in real-time, but chatbots can answer common questions and provide assistance even when your staff are unavailable. The good news is, Artificial Intelligence is progressing so fast that ultra-low-cost chatbots are becoming affordable for just about every business.

And of course, the golden opportunity is to offer online payment options on your website to make it more convenient for clients to purchase products and services. By selling skincare products or gift cards and allowing clients to pre-pay for treatments, you can increase revenue, remove the risk of no-shows and improve client retention. When implementing e-commerce solutions, consider the following:

■   **Secure payment processing:** Choose a reputable payment gateway, such as Stripe, PayPal, or Worldpay, to ensure secure and reliable transactions that your clients will trust.
■   **Inventory management:** If you sell products too, select an e-commerce

platform that allows you to manage stock levels and track sales easily. Popular options include Shopify, WooCommerce, and BigCommerce.

- **Shipping and delivery:** If selling physical products, set up shipping options and costs for your clients. Ensure you have a clear return policy in place.
- **Product descriptions and images:** Invest time in creating compelling product descriptions and high-quality images to showcase your products and services effectively.

Finally, giving clients the ability to **create and manage their accounts** on your website can foster loyalty and streamline their experience. By offering a client portal, you can allow clients to update their contact details, ensuring your database remains up-to-date; view past and upcoming appointments, making it easier for them to remember and reschedule them if necessary (reducing the burden on your admin too); and give them the comfort of access to their payment history or outstanding balances.

For a really engaging service, you can also give them access to personalised treatment plans and an idea of their progress, which will also help you to upsell future treatments. Be sure to implement secure login procedures and data protection measures to safeguard your clients' personal information.

ANALYTICS AND PERFORMANCE TRACKING

There's one more bit of back-end functionality to add to your website. To make informed decisions about your marketing efforts and website improvements, it's essential to track your website's performance. Integrating analytics tools, such as Google Analytics, will provide valuable insights into:

- **Website traffic:** Monitor the number of visitors, the source of traffic, and the most visited pages on your website.

- **User behaviour:** Analyse how visitors interact with your website, including time spent on each page, bounce rate, and conversion rates.
- **Campaign performance:** Measure the effectiveness of your marketing campaigns, such as email marketing, social media, and paid advertising.
- **SEO performance:** Track keyword rankings and organic search traffic to identify areas for improvement and growth.

> "Web analytics is a fire extinguisher.
> Your website is on fire and you're burning cash."
>
> JIM STERNE, DIGITAL MARKETING EXPERT AND
> FOUNDER OF THE EMETRICS SUMMIT

By regularly reviewing and analysing this data, you can identify trends, areas for improvement, and opportunities to better serve your clients and grow your practice. If you use a marketing agency, they will take care of all the analytics for you.

CHECKLIST

☑ Define your core values – the principles that set your aesthetics practice apart from competitors.

☑ Discover your Unique Selling Proposition (USP).

☑ Create a consistent visual identity – logo, colour palette, typography, etc.

☑ Create a compelling brand story.

continued

☑ Build a user-friendly website – easy to navigate, visually appealing, and mobile-responsive.

☑ Optimize your website's performance.

☑ Ensure website accessibility: make your site accessible to all users, including those with disabilities, by using clear language, alt text for images, and keyboard navigation.

☑ Create high-quality, relevant content addressing target audience needs.

☑ Provide contact information.

☑ Perform keyword research to identify target keywords.

☑ Build high-quality backlinks to increase credibility and authority.

☑ Promote content on social media to drive traffic and visibility.

☑ Monitor SEO performance regularly using tools like Google Analytics.

☑ Implement advanced website functionality (e.g., online booking, live chat, e-commerce).

☑ Integrate social media into your website for increased visibility and engagement.

☑ Offer online payment options for convenience and increased revenue.

☑ Consider working with a marketing agency to help manage analytics and performance tracking.

KEEPING AN EYE
ON THE WORLD

If you've read this far, you'll have realised that I obsess over research in marketing. That's because actually doing marketing costs money, and money which doesn't bring customers through the door is money literally wasted.

The good news is, the internet is great at research, and several research websites can help you understand the audience for your business.

Here are some popular tools and platforms that can provide valuable insights; I think we can split them into two classes: understanding audience trends (what your customers care about) and understanding keyword trends (what works and what doesn't, based on statistical analysis of multiple websites' performance).

"Don't find customers for your products,
find products for your customers."

MARKETING GURU, SETH GODIN

AUDIENCE TRENDS

- **AnswerThePublic (answerthepublic.com):** I think AnswerThePublic is a marketer's secret weapon! It's an online keyword research tool that generates visual reports of popular questions and phrases people search for around a given topic. By entering a keyword or phrase, the tool fetches data from search engines like Google and Bing, presenting it in a visually appealing format, such as a question wheel or categorized lists. These insights help marketers to understand the exact questions that customers are asking, helping you to identify content gaps, and create relevant content that addresses those queries, ultimately improving your search engine visibility and user engagement.

- **Quora (quora.com):** Quora is a question-and-answer platform where you can search for questions related to your industry or niche. By analyzing questions and answers about aesthetics, for example, you can understand the pain points and interests of your target audience.

- **Reddit (reddit.com):** Reddit is a platform that hosts numerous topic-specific forums called subreddits. By searching for subreddits about aesthetics and engaging in discussions, you can gain insights into your audience's opinions and preferences, and even build new relevant relationships. It will also help you to build your profile as an industry expert.

KEYWORD TRENDS

- **Google Trends (trends.google.com):** Google Trends allows you to explore search trends and compare the popularity of different keywords over time. This can help you identify the topics your customers are most interested in and tailor your content accordingly.

- **SEMrush (semrush.com):** SEMrush is a comprehensive SEO and marketing tool that provides insights into your competitors' strategies and helps you identify potential gaps in your target audience's needs. You can analyze keywords, backlinks, and content performance to optimize your marketing efforts.

■ **SimilarWeb (similarweb.com):** SimilarWeb offers website analytics and competitive intelligence, allowing you to compare your website's performance with your competitors. By analyzing your competitors' traffic sources, audience demographics, and engagement metrics, you can gain a better understanding of your own audience's preferences.

■ **Social media and Google Analytics:** Search engines and social media platforms, such as Google Analytics, Facebook Insights, Twitter Analytics, and Instagram Insights, provide detailed analytics on your followers and their engagement with your content. By analyzing these metrics, you can understand your audience's preferences and tailor your strategy accordingly.

All of these resources will help you gather valuable information about your customers, allowing you to create more targeted and effective marketing strategies.

CHECKLIST

☑ Use AnswerThePublic to identify popular questions and phrases related to your niche.

☑ Explore Quora to understand pain points and interests of your target audience.

☑ Engage in Reddit discussions to gain insights and build your profile as an industry expert.

☑ Use Google Trends to explore search trends and tailor your content accordingly.

☑ Analyze competitors' performance with SimilarWeb for a better understanding of your audience.

☑ Use social media and Google Analytics to track follower engagement and preferences.

CONTENT MARKETING

Content marketing is the part of marketing that involves creating and sharing material online (videos, blogs, social media posts, etc.) that does not explicitly promote a brand (that's advertising) but instead stimulates interest by showing expertise or building rapport.

As an aesthetics practice, having a robust content marketing strategy will therefore help you to attract potential clients, retain existing ones, and establish yourself as an authority in the industry. By creating and sharing valuable, informative, and engaging content, you can enhance your online presence and connect with your audience. In this section, we'll explore various types of content and discuss when to use each one to effectively market your operation.

Websites with active and frequent blog content have a 434% higher chance of ranking top of Google for key search terms, according to a 2019 survey by HubSpot. The same survey found that websites with blogs on average receive 67% more enquiries than those that do not have blog content.

TYPES OF CONTENT AND WHEN TO USE THEM

- **Blog Posts:** Blog posts are the backbone of content marketing, as they allow you to share your expertise, discuss industry trends, and in particular, address common client concerns. They are a cost-effective way to improve your website's search engine visibility and drive organic traffic. In aesthetics, particularly good subjects include:

  - ☐ **Informational content:** Share insights into treatments and skincare routines to educate and inform your audience.
  - ☐ **Case studies:** Showcase the success stories of your clients, detailing the treatments they received and their results.
  - ☐ **"Listicles"**, aka "Top 5s" and "Top 10s": Compile lists of tips, product recommendations, or treatment options that are easily digestible and shareable (they're also easy to write).
  - ☐ **Expert interviews:** Collaborate with industry experts to create insightful, in-depth content that appeals to your customer and also has the credibility of being advice from someone else.

- **Infographics:** Infographics are a visually engaging way to present complex information or data in an easy-to-understand format. They are particularly effective for breaking down complicated procedures, highlighting statistics, or providing step-by-step guides. They're also highly shareable and can feature your logo/brand, which is handy. Infographics used to cost quite a lot to produce, but the tools now are so advanced that it's within the realm of an evening's work to produce something quite exciting. Consider creating infographics to:

  - ☐ **Visualize treatment processes:** Help clients understand what to expect during specific procedures by illustrating the steps involved.

☐ **Share skincare tips:** Provide advice on skincare routines, product usage, or treatment aftercare in a visually appealing manner.

☐ **Compare treatment options:** Help clients make informed decisions by visually comparing the pros and cons of different treatments.

■ **Videos:** Videos are an unbelievably popular content format today, partly thanks to the popularity of TikTok and Reels. They provide an immersive, dynamic way to showcase your work as they allow you to demonstrate treatments, share testimonials, and address common concerns, all with the authenticity of a real person. Good video ideas include:

☐ **Treatment demonstrations:** Offer a behind-the-scenes look at your practice by showcasing treatments and procedures in action.

☐ **Client testimonials:** Share the experiences of satisfied clients, emphasizing the positive impact your treatments have had on their lives.

☐ **Q&A sessions:** Address common questions or concerns by responding to client inquiries in a video format.

☐ **Educational content:** Provide detailed explanations of treatments, aftercare tips or industry trends to position yourself as an expert in the field.

■ **Social Media Content:** Honestly, social media platforms like Instagram, Facebook, and Twitter are no longer a "nice to have". They're essential. The good news is, you can post as regularly or irregularly as you want, and creating material can take minutes, not days. Create platform-specific content to increase your online visibility and foster a sense of community around your practice. Ideas for social media content include:

- ☐ **Before and after images:** Showcase the results of your treatments by sharing visual transformations.
- ☐ **Behind-the-scenes glimpses:** Offer a sneak peek into your practice, highlighting your team, facilities, and the treatments you provide.
- ☐ **Tips and advice:** Share bite-sized tips and treatment information.
- ☐ **Promotions and events:** Keep your audience up to date with special offers, upcoming events, or new treatments available at your practice.

■ **E-books and Guides:** E-books and downloadable guides are the opposite of your social media activity. They're all about credibility, allowing you to provide your customers with in-depth, valuable information that they can access on demand. These resources can be used as 'lead magnets' to grow your email list (i.e. they're informative enough that customers will happily surrender their email addresses to be able to download the guide) or as educational material for clients. Consider creating e-books on:

- ☐ **Comprehensive treatment guides:** Dive deep into specific treatments, explaining the process, benefits, potential side effects, and aftercare instructions. This can help clients make informed decisions about their aesthetic treatments.
- ☐ **Skincare routines:** Provide detailed advice on daily skincare routines, product recommendations, and tips for various skin types and concerns.
- ☐ **Pre- and post-treatment care:** Educate clients on the necessary steps to prepare for treatments and to ensure optimal results, as well as guidelines for post-treatment care and recovery.

■ **Podcasts:** Podcasts offer an engaging, conversational and intensely human way to share expertise, and connect with your audience. By creating a podcast, you can showcase your practice's personality and build trust with potential clients. Powerful topics include:

- ☐ **Expert interviews:** Invite industry experts or fellow practitioners to discuss their experiences, share insights, and offer advice to your listeners.
- ☐ **Treatment deep dives:** Dedicate episodes to specific treatments, providing in-depth information and answering common questions.
- ☐ **Client stories:** Share inspiring stories of clients who have undergone transformative treatments at your practice, focusing on their journey and outcomes.
- ☐ **Industry news and developments:** Discuss the latest advancements in aesthetics, exploring their potential impact on clients and the industry as a whole.

What does all this tell us? Most obviously, you can see that different subjects are appropriate for different types of media. And there's an overlap – subjects can be covered in more than one medium. The other big lesson is that you can't do everything. You should get into the habit of regular social media posts; plus the occasional blog when it demonstrably makes sense to do so. Anything else is icing on the cake – find a couple of activities you enjoy and stick to that. It's better to do one or two media activities well than to try to do everything and do them all badly.

One more thing: whatever you produce, get maximum value from each activity by promoting it everywhere. If you produce a podcast interview, for example, put the transcript into a blog and send a link to it in your email newsletter. Produce once, promote ten times.

YOUR CONTENT STRATEGY

That brings us to content strategy. Strategy ensures that the content you create is targeted, relevant, and engaging for your audience – so that it doesn't waste their time, or yours. In this section, we'll discuss the key components of a content strategy, including making content shareable, establishing a publishing schedule, and more.

"Your customers don't care about you, your products, or your services. They care about themselves."

JOE PULIZZI, FOUNDER, THE CONTENT MARKETING INSTITUTE

Start by outlining the goals and objectives of your content marketing efforts. Typical goals for aesthetics practices include increasing brand awareness, attracting new clients, developing client trust and loyalty, and ultimately positioning your practice as an industry expert.

To create content that resonates with your audience, you need to understand their needs. Above, we looked at the thought and market research work required to understand customer preferences and pain points. You should already have effective buyer personas in mind to help guide your content creation process. If not, head back to Chapter 2 and get comfortable with your customer base!

Before developing new content, take stock of the content you already have. Analyse your existing content to determine what's working well, what could be improved, and what gaps need to be filled. This will help you identify opportunities for new content (not just gap-fillers, but also further materials based on the subjects that your customers are actually interested in) and ensure that you're not duplicating effort.

Then get to work. Develop a diverse mix of content types to engage your audience and cater to their varying preferences. As discussed in the previous section, consider incorporating blog posts, infographics, videos, social media content, e-books, guides, and podcasts into your content strategy. Tailor your content mix to your audience, ensuring that it addresses their needs and interests. But as we also saw above, stick to what you can meaningfully achieve – month after month – in your already busy schedule. Again, do a few things well, not a lot of things badly!

That's because consistency is key in content marketing. Define a publishing schedule to ensure that you're regularly creating and sharing fresh content with your audience. That means:

- **Frequency:** Determine how often you'll publish new content, based on your resources and availability, audience preferences and material available. Aim for a balance between quality and quantity.
- **Timing:** Identify the optimal times to share content on each platform. Email newsletters, for example, seem to work best when sent on Tuesday afternoons; there is platform-specific best practice available online, free of charge, for almost every media opportunity.
- **Content themes:** Organize your content around themes or topics to make it easier to plan and create a cohesive content strategy.

One of the primary goals of content marketing is to reach a wider audience. To achieve this, your content needs to be shareable. Create engaging, rich, high-quality content that provides real value to your audience. Not everything needs to be a work of art, but good visuals and elegant branding will certainly help. Incorporate eye-catching images, infographics, and videos to make your content instantly appealing. Craft attention-grabbing headlines that encourage users to click in the first place, and then share your content afterwards. That comes with a bit of a warning too – typical clickbait headings like "You won't believe what happened next in this threading consultation" aren't going to do your reputation any good at all! Finally, include social sharing buttons on your blog posts and web pages, enabling users to share your content with just a few clicks.

One more thing on content strategy. We took a look above at SEO (if you missed it, head back up for a full examination of SEO techniques). When you create new content, you want it to be SEO-optimised too. So use all the techniques above, in particular inserting powerful keywords and incorporating internal and external links that connect you to other credible corners of the internet. And above all, use metadata – the title, description and other tagging information which helps search engines to understand what your content is about.

Keep in mind that a successful content strategy is an ongoing process demanding regular review and continuous refinement to ensure that your content stays relevant and engaging for your audience.

SO HOW DID WE DO?

Measuring the effectiveness of your content is a critical part of your content marketing strategy. It allows you to determine the success of your efforts and means you can make reliable, data-driven decisions, and refine your content to better resonate with your audience. In this section, we'll discuss some of the key metrics and analytics tools you should use. It's worth allowing some time for your marketing activities to bed down, and if you use an agency, they will be pleased to do the analytics for you; but it's worth keeping an eye on your stats once a month or so.

Choosing the right key performance indicators (KPIs) for your content marketing efforts will depend on what you actually want to achieve, but there are some common general KPIs to look out for:

- **Traffic:** This metric tracks the number of visitors to your website, blog, or social media pages. It therefore indicates the reach of your content and helps you determine which content is driving the most visitor interest. If you look at nothing else, this should be your first port of call.
- **Engagement:** Engagement metrics measure how your audience is interacting with your content. Think about likes, shares and comments

on social posts, and the time spent on pages of content. If users arrive on a page but only spend a few seconds there, for example, that suggests that they are excited enough about a subject to come to your page, but disappointed enough that it hasn't met their expectations and they decided to go somewhere else. Engagement metrics thus help you understand how your audience is responding to your content and which content is resonating with them the most.

- **Conversions:** Conversions measure the number of leads or sales generated as a result of your content marketing efforts. If the amount of traffic to your website remains the same, but the amount of business you achieve increases, then that's a higher conversion rate and a sign that your content is performing well.

Working these stats out is a profession in itself, and I've mentioned elsewhere that it's something an agency is probably best placed to do on your behalf. If you do decide to assess your performance metrics yourself, all platforms have some form of analytics tools. The most common are as follows, but note that they all perform differently, and it can take some time to navigate around them comfortably:

- **Google Analytics:** Google Analytics is the leading free web analytics tool providing valuable insights into your website's performance. It allows you to track website traffic, user behaviour and conversion rates. You can also set up custom reports to track the performance of each piece of content you produce, and it's easy to set up, too.
- **Social Media Analytics:** Most social media platforms provide built-in analytics tools that allow you to track the performance of your social media content, such as likes, shares, comments, and click-through rates.
- **Content Management Systems (CMS):** A CMS is a system which manages your website (we've mentioned Wix, Squarespace and WordPress above). Most content management systems offer built-in

analytics tools that allow you to track the performance of your content. On WordPress, you can buy low-cost plugins which will add further dimensions to your analytics if appropriate.

- **Email Marketing Analytics:** Email marketing platforms, such as Mailchimp and ConstantContact, provide tools to track the performance of your email campaigns. Look for insights like open rates (how many people opened your email), click-through rates (how many people then clicked on a story to return to your website), and conversion metrics (how many of those clicks then turned into new business).

Let's conclude with some basic advice for interpreting metrics, because a bunch of numbers is…just a bunch of numbers. First, wherever possible, use a combination of metrics to measure the effectiveness of your content. This will give you a more complete picture of how it is performing and help you identify any areas for improvement. Second, track your metrics over time, because it's the trends and patterns that will give you the insight you can actually act on. Measuring the effectiveness of your content is an ongoing process. Finally, if you can compare your results to benchmarks as well as your own historical performance, you'll get even closer to interpreting the raw data more meaningfully.

Then, it's about incremental improvement. Refine your content and adjust your strategy accordingly, for small but continuous increases in the value of your marketing activity.

BUT I CAN'T DO IT . . .

One more thing. In my experience with aesthetics professionals, I consistently come up against excuses for not creating content. Many people think they're not good enough. But every day, you create artistry with a needle and some filler. Writing some content or recording a video is truly a piece of cake compared to that. And you really do know what you're talking about: you prove that every day with patients – the only difference here is you are now documenting it. Put the same commitment into content creation that you put into your everyday work and you will make a difference.

I also speak to practitioners who are fearful of being judged. But if you think about it, your fear is not of being judged by patients or potential patients, but by fellow practitioners. And they don't matter – this is about you and your patients alone. So just get started, and I promise you won't look back!

CHECKLIST

☑ Define your content marketing goals and objectives.

☑ Analyze your existing content and identify opportunities for improvement or new content.

☑ Identify the best types of content for your audience and practice: blogs, infographics, videos, social media, e-books, or podcasts.

☑ Focus on one or two content formats you enjoy and can consistently create, rather than attempting to cover all formats.

☑ Create shareable content with eye-catching visuals, engaging headlines, and social sharing buttons.

☑ Establish a consistent publishing schedule.

☑ Use your content formats to share expertise, address client concerns, showcase treatments, and provide other valuable information.

☑ Optimize your content for SEO, using keywords, internal and external links, and metadata.

continued

☑ Repurpose and promote your content across different platforms to maximize its reach.

☑ Update your social media platforms regularly with relevant and engaging content.

☑ Use lead magnets, like e-books and guides, to grow your email list.

☑ Allow time for your marketing activities to settle in

☑ Continuously monitor the performance of your content and adjust your strategy accordingly.

EMAIL MARKETING

Email isn't cool. But while Instagram may get all the credit, email marketing remains a devastatingly effective way to connect with existing clients and attract new ones. How many email newsletters and promotions do you still get every day? Exactly. Email is still gold, and building a quality email list is the foundation of any successful email marketing campaign. Let's start there.

According to email software business, Campaign Monitor, the average open rate for emails in the healthcare sector is 23.7%.

HTTPS://WWW.CAMPAIGNMONITOR.COM/RESOURCES/GUIDES/
EMAIL-MARKETING-BENCHMARKS/

THE LEGAL FRAMEWORK

Before you begin building your email list, it's essential to familiarize yourself with the legal requirements for owners of mailing lists. The General Data Protection Regulation (GDPR) and the Privacy and Electronic Communications Regulations (PECR) govern the collection, processing, and use of personal data in email marketing. Here are the key principles you need to be mindful of:

- **Consent:** To send marketing emails, you must have explicit consent from the individual. This means they must actively opt-in to receive your emails. Pre-ticked boxes, silence, or inactivity do not constitute consent.
- **Transparency:** Individuals must be clearly informed about how their data will be used, who it will be shared with, and their right to withdraw consent at any time. You should put all this information in your privacy policy and provide a link to it when collecting personal information.
- **Data Minimization:** You may only collect the data necessary to fulfil the purpose for which it was collected. For email marketing, this typically includes a name and email address; although you would have no trouble standing up in court to justify collecting e.g. the five things which most interested a client. What you can't do is collect everyone's inside leg measurement for no reason.
- **Data Security:** You must store personal data securely and protect it against unauthorized access, disclosure, or destruction.

BUILD AN EMAIL LIST

Now that you understand the legal framework, it's time to start building your list. One of the most effective ways to encourage sign-ups is by offering something valuable in exchange for an email address. Here are some ideas to get you started:

- **Exclusive promotions:** Offer potential clients a discount or a special offer on their first treatment when they sign up for your email list. This is super easy to do.
- **Educational content:** Create a free e-book, video series, or webinar on a relevant topic, e.g. anti-ageing treatments or the science behind popular aesthetics procedures. Provide access to this content in exchange for an email address. This is harder because you actually have to write the e-book.

- **Newsletter:** Curate a newsletter featuring industry news, tips and updates on your clinic's offerings. Promote it on your website, social media channels, and in your clinic, highlighting the benefits of subscribing. This is also easy to do. Don't commit to a monthly newsletter because you'll have to write it every month. Nobody is expecting something every month. Instead, write a newsletter when you've got something great to talk about. It'll be much easier.

As you can see, all of these demand some sort of sign-up form, where the user/reader can give their email address. Keep these forms simple: limit the number of fields in your form to avoid overwhelming potential subscribers. Generally, just ask for a name and email address. Use clear call-to-action buttons (CTA in marketing jargon)– these are the signposts that tell a user how to sign up. Make your CTA buttons stand out with contrasting colours and use simple text. We'd love to make this more exciting, but "Sign Up" or "Subscribe Now" are absolutely the way to go. Put your sign-up forms in prominent locations on your website, such as the homepage, the header, the footer, or in a sidebar. Consider using a pop-up form that appears after a visitor has spent a certain amount of time on your site (this is an off-the-shelf piece of functionality in WordPress, for example).

Social media platforms are also a valuable tool for building your email list. Share snippets of your newsletter content or promotional offers on your social media channels, along with a link to your sign-up form. This will allow you to add value to your social viewers while promoting at the same time. Add a sign-up tab or link to your email list on your Facebook page, encouraging your followers to subscribe.

You might also run targeted ads promoting your exclusive offers or educational content, driving users to a landing page where they can sign up for your email list. This will obviously attract a cost, but it may be worth buying subscribers if your conversion rate is high enough (see metrics, below in this chapter).

Finally, don't forget to collect email addresses from clients visiting your clinic in person! Train your staff to ask for clients' email addresses during the check-in process. Explain the benefits of joining your email list, such as exclusive offers and valuable tips. Remember, the fact that someone has surrendered their email address while making an online booking does not automatically mean that they have consented to a newsletter, unless this is made clear as part of the booking process. But if you welcome them personally and gain permission for use of the email at the reception desk, that's a perfectly legitimate way to go.

You might also consider placing a sign-up sheet (a bit old-school...) or an iPad with a digital sign-up form (much sexier) in your waiting area. Encourage clients to subscribe to your newsletter while they wait for their appointment.

Email marketing has the highest return on investment for small businesses.

HTTPS://WWW.HUBSPOT.COM/MARKETING-STATISTICS

There are a couple more strong but indirect ways to get email sign-ups and initial sales contacts.

A referral program can be an effective way to expand your email list. Offer incentives to your existing clients for referring friends or family members who sign up for your email list. For example, you could provide a discount on their next (or first) treatment, a free product, or a gift card. This not only helps you grow your list but also encourages client loyalty.

Partnering with complementary businesses, such as beauty brands, fitness studios, or other salons, can help you reach new audiences. Consider co-hosting events, and webinars, or creating joint offers that require participants to sign up for both your email lists. This can be a mutually beneficial arrangement, as both businesses will gain exposure to new potential clients.

COMPELLING CONTENT: CRAFTING EMAIL CAMPAIGNS IN AESTHETICS

Once you've built a solid email list, the next step is to create engaging and effective email campaigns that add value to your audience. The success of your email campaigns largely depends on the content you provide. The key types of content that work are very similar to those we discuss in Chapter 9, below (Social Media):

■ **Educational articles:** Share insights on skincare routines, the latest aesthetics treatments, or tips for maintaining post-treatment results. By the way, by "Educational", we don't mean preachy, or even specifically marking content as educational. So long as your customers feel more informed than they were before, this is a winning formula.

■ **Client success stories:** Showcase before-and-after photos and testimonials from satisfied clients to build trust and demonstrate the effectiveness of your treatments.

■ **Exclusive promotions:** Offer time-sensitive deals or special packages available only to your email subscribers, creating a sense of exclusivity and urgency.

■ **Clinic news and updates:** Make the housekeeping interesting! Keep your clients informed about new treatments, staff additions, or upcoming events at your practice.

Whatever content you choose to cover, we have to call out the most important piece of content in an email: the subject line. It's the first thing your recipient will see and often determines whether they'll open your email or dismiss it like so many others. Create attention-grabbing subject lines by following these tips:

■ **Keep it short and sweet:** Aim for subject lines between 6-10 words. Long subject lines may get cut off, particularly on mobile devices.

- **Be clear and specific:** Communicate the value of your email content to encourage recipients to open it. You may only have two seconds to make an impact.
- **Personalize it:** Include the recipient's name or reference a specific treatment they may be interested in to make your email feel more tailored. Most email management systems will allow you to insert variables (e.g. "[FIRSTNAME], discover dermal fillers") into your subject line and copy.
- **Use action words:** Encourage action with verbs like "discover," "learn," or "save."
- **Test emojis:** Emojis can add a touch of personality and make your subject line stand out. Use them sparingly.

As you've probably realised here, above all, email newsletters and promotions shouldn't be complicated. They don't need ten different stories, and they don't need complex visual flourishes. Simplicity works far better. That is true for the design of the newsletter as well as for the content. A well-designed email with clear formatting not only looks professional but will also be much more readable. Use a responsive email template that adapts to different screen sizes, so that both desktop and mobile users get a seamless reading experience. Stick to a simple layout with clear headings, short paragraphs, and bullet points for easy scanning. Incorporate visuals like images and videos to break up text and add visual interest. And, of course, use consistent branding elements including your logo, colour scheme and fonts to reinforce your brand identity. But don't let it get finicky!

YOUR SOFTWARE OPTIONS

We've mentioned software a couple of times already, so let's take a moment to think about choosing the right software. If you're managing your own campaigns, consider the following factors:

- **Ease of use:** Look for a platform with an intuitive user interface, making it simple for you and your team to create and manage email campaigns.
- **List management:** You need a platform that allows you to easily segment and manage your email list, enabling you to target specific groups of clients with tailored content. Most will also allow you to manage sign-ups to ensure that you can demonstrably stay on the right side of the law (see above)
- **Templates:** Choose software that offers a variety of responsive, customizable templates off-the-shelf to ensure your emails look professional and adapt to different screen sizes.
- **Automation capabilities:** Automated features, such as autoresponders, welcome email sequences, and drip campaigns, can save time and streamline your marketing efforts.
- **Reporting and analytics:** Comprehensive reporting tools are essential for tracking the performance of your email campaigns.
- **Integration with other tools:** Ensure your chosen platform can integrate with your existing CRM, website, and social media platforms to create a cohesive marketing ecosystem.
- **Pricing:** Finally, of course, compare pricing plans among different software options, taking into account factors like the size of your email list, the number of emails you plan to send, and the features you require. It would be lovely if email software came at easily comparable price points, but it doesn't: the big players generally set fees according to various different measures from this list.

Here are a few popular email marketing platforms that cater to businesses of all sizes, including the smaller practice:

- **Mailchimp:** Very much the default (and not in a bad way). Known for its user-friendly interface and extensive template library, Mailchimp is an excellent option for businesses new to email marketing. It offers automation features, analytics, and a free plan for smaller email lists.

- **Sendinblue** is a powerful platform that provides email and SMS marketing tools, automation capabilities, and advanced segmentation options. It offers a free plan with limited features and various paid plans to accommodate growing businesses.
- **Constant Contact:** With its robust email marketing features, including automation, list management, and reporting tools, Constant Contact is a popular choice for small to medium-sized businesses. It also offers a website builder and e-commerce integration, which might be of interest if you're bundling your needs together.
- **GetResponse:** Again, combines email marketing with a suite of marketing tools, including landing page builders, webinars, and CRM functionality. Its automation and personalization features make it an attractive option for growing aesthetics practices.

METRICS: MEASURING EMAIL MARKETING SUCCESS

Tracking and analyzing the performance of your email marketing campaigns is essential for understanding the effectiveness of your effort and spend. To evaluate the success of your email marketing efforts, here are the metrics you should monitor:

- **Open rate:** The percentage of recipients who opened your email. This metric will help you gauge the effectiveness of your subject lines and sender name.
- **Click-through rate (CTR):** The percentage of recipients who clicked on a link within your email. CTR is an indicator of how engaging your content is and whether your call-to-actions (CTAs) are effective.
- **Conversion rate:** The percentage of recipients who completed a desired action after clicking a link in your email, such as booking a treatment or purchasing a product. This metric demonstrates the overall effectiveness of your email in driving desired outcomes.
- **Bounce rate:** The percentage of emails that were not delivered, either

due to a temporary issue (soft bounce) or an invalid email address (hard bounce). High bounce rates may signal issues with your email list or potential deliverability problems.

- **Unsubscribe rate:** The percentage of recipients who opted out of your email list after receiving your campaign. A high unsubscribe rate suggests that your content really isn't resonating with your audience or possibly that you're sending emails too frequently.

Most email marketing platforms provide built-in analytics dashboards that display these key metrics for each of your campaigns in real-time. Log in to your email marketing platform and navigate to the analytics or reporting section; select the specific campaign you want to analyze, and you'll be able to review pre-designed metrics and charts to assess the performance of your campaign with little or no effort. You can then usually also export this data to a spreadsheet or generate custom reports for more in-depth analysis or to compare multiple campaigns.

What sort of custom reports? Well, if you really want to earn your email marketing chops, you might like to experiment with A/B Testing. Also known as "split testing", A/B testing involves sending two versions of an email to a small segment of your list to determine which performs better (that's why your reports and stats matter). Once you've identified the winner, you'll then send that version to the remainder of your list. A/B testing thus helps you optimize your email campaigns by identifying what emails work best with your audience.

With basic A/B testing, your criteria can include almost anything creative:

- **Subject lines:** Experiment with different wording, personalization, or emojis to see what drives higher open rates.
- **Email content:** Test different types of content to see what engages your audience.

- **Visuals:** Compare the impact of different images, videos, or graphics on click-through rates and conversions.
- **Call-to-action (CTA) buttons:** Test variations in colour, text, and placement to find the most effective combination.

Note, importantly, that one A/B test – particularly on visuals and CTAs – can give you an insight that you can put to work for six months or more. It's frankly a bit of a faff for a smaller practice but can be incredibly effective in increasing your email response rates.

More simply, use the insights gained from your metrics every couple of months (or after every major campaign) to refine and improve your campaign design:

- **Subject lines:** If your open rates are low, experiment with different subject line styles, phrasing and personalizations to capture your audience's attention.
- **Enhance content and CTAs:** If your CTR is low, consider revising your content to make it more engaging, adjusting the design for better readability, or testing different CTA styles and placements.
- **Segment your audience:** Tailor your content to specific segments of your email list based on factors like past treatments, demographics, or engagement patterns. This can help increase relevancy, boost engagement, and reduce unsubscribe rates (but it does, of course, mean having more than one version of your email).
- **Clean your email list:** Take some time to regularly remove hard bounces (if they're not automatically removed by your email software), inactive subscribers, or invalid email addresses from your list to maintain high deliverability rates and improve the accuracy of your metrics.
- **Adjust sending frequency:** If your unsubscribe rate is high, consider reducing the frequency of your emails or experimenting with different sending schedules to find the optimal balance for your audience.

In fact, let's take a moment to look at send frequencies, because this is always challenging. It's best practice to communicate your sending frequency because this helps manage expectations and reduces the likelihood of subscribers feeling overwhelmed or annoyed by your emails. I think this is good advice at the sign-up stage, inasmuch as it's good to set a maximum, e.g. "We won't email you more than once per fortnight".

However, nobody is sitting around waiting for a newsletter from any business. So please don't feel you have to commit to "our monthly email". It's much better to only send emails out when you've got something interesting to say, not to commit to an entirely unnecessary frequency, and furthermore to make sure you don't spend your evenings writing pointless emails.

Given all that, start with a moderate frequency to avoid overwhelming your subscribers and your own head. As you gather more data on engagement and unsubscribe rates, you can adjust your send frequency accordingly. To do this, keep a close eye on your open, click-through, and unsubscribe rates to gauge how your audience responds to your email frequency. If you notice a spike in unsubscribes or a decline in engagement, consider reducing the number of emails you send. And you can always A/B test on frequencies, too: experiment with different sending frequencies for specific segments of your list to identify the optimal communication rate.

MORE TIPS FOR THE BLACK BELT EMAIL MARKETER

To further enhance your email marketing efforts, consider these additional tips:

- **Test your emails across devices:** Ensure your emails render correctly on various devices and email clients by testing them before sending. Many email marketing platforms offer preview tools to help with this process.

- **Use a consistent sender name:** A consistent sender name and email address will build trust and familiarity with your recipients. This could be your practice name or the name of a specific staff member, for example.
- **Encourage engagement:** Invite your subscribers to respond to your emails or share them on social media by including clear CTAs and social sharing buttons. This can help you gather valuable feedback, spread awareness about your practice, and grow your email list.
- **Monitor and adjust, monitor and adjust, monitor and adjust again....:** Like almost everything in marketing, this is an incremental science. Continuously review the performance of your email campaigns and use the insights from your metrics to optimize your content, design, subject lines, and send frequency.

CHECKLIST

☑ Familiarize yourself with the legal framework (GDPR and PECR) for email marketing.

☑ Build an email list by offering valuable incentives and using sign-up forms.

☑ Use social media platforms to promote your email list and expand your audience.

☑ Collect email addresses from clients visiting your clinic in person.

☑ Consider implementing a referral program to grow your email list.

☑ Create compelling email campaigns with engaging content.

☑ Choose the right email marketing software: consider ease of use, list management, templates, automation, reporting, integration, and pricing.

☑ Use automation features to save time.

☑ Track key metrics like open rate, click-through rate (CTR), conversion rate, bounce rate and unsubscribe rate.

☑ Perform A/B testing: Experiment with different subject lines, content, visuals, and call-to-action (CTA) buttons to optimize your email campaigns.

☑ Keep a clean email list: regularly remove hard bounces, inactive subscribers, and invalid email addresses for better deliverability rates and metric accuracy.

☑ Focus on quality over quantity.

Don't leave just yet! I know you have to pay for online ads, but they have become something of an integral part of the marketing strategy for businesses across various industries, and aesthetics is no exception. Harnessing the power of online advertising can help you reach a broader audience, improve brand visibility, and ultimately, increase your revenue. And more importantly, because money is at stake, the advertising industry has developed to be obsessive about showing value. Compared to everything else I've written about here, you're going to get a better idea of your return on investment from ads than from anything else you do.

Still here? Good! In this section, we'll look at all the major online advertising platforms in the UK, delving into the benefits, usability, software, reach, and functionality of each. By the end of this chapter, you'll have a comprehensive understanding of the main options, allowing you to make informed decisions when implementing an online advertising strategy for your aesthetics practice.

THE PLATFORMS

Google Ads is the world's largest and most popular online advertising platform, known for its wide reach, powerful targeting capabilities, and ease of use. As a search engine giant, Google receives billions of searches every day, making it an invaluable platform for businesses looking to target potential customers based on nuanced search queries. Bing is catching up, but there really is no substitute for the Big G:

- **Wide reach:** With Google's vast user base, your advertisements can reach a broad audience, increasing the chances of attracting potential clients.
- **Targeting capabilities:** Google Ads offers a multitude of targeting options, including keywords, demographics, interests, and geographical locations (I'll come back to geography in the next chapter), allowing you to display your ads to the most relevant audience.
- **Cost-effective:** Google Ads uses a pay-per-click (PPC) model, meaning you only pay when someone clicks on your ad. This makes it a cost-effective option for small to medium-sized businesses.
- **Usability and Software:** Google Ads provides an intuitive interface, which makes it easy for users to navigate and manage their ad campaigns. The platform offers a range of tools and resources, such as the Google Ads Editor, which simplifies the process of creating, editing, and optimising ads.

Google Ads offers multiple ad types, including search ads, display ads, video ads and shopping ads, providing flexibility in terms of how your advertisements appear. Its extensive reach, combined with its targeting capabilities, makes it a highly effective first platform for new advertisers looking to mop up a large chunk of the addressable audience fairly flexibly.

Facebook Ads is the other truly major player in the online advertising space, allowing businesses to leverage the power of the world's largest social media platform to reach potential clients. With over 2.8 billion monthly active users globally, Facebook Ads offers businesses the opportunity to target a wide audience based on an intensely granular understanding of demographics, interests, and behaviour.

- **Extensive targeting options:** Similar to Google Ads, Facebook Ads provides a wide range of targeting options, allowing you to tailor your ads to the most relevant audience, particularly by their interests.
- **Multiple ad formats:** Facebook Ad formats include photo, video, carousel, slideshow, and collection ads, allowing for creative flexibility in how you present your aesthetics practice to potential clients.
- **Integration with Instagram:** Facebook Ads is seamlessly integrated with Instagram (the company Meta owns both platforms), enabling you to run ads on both platforms simultaneously and expand your reach even further for relatively low additional effort.
- **Usability and Software:** Facebook Ads Manager, the primary tool for creating and managing ad campaigns on the platform, features a user-friendly interface that makes it easy to set up, monitor, and optimise your ads. Additionally, Facebook offers several resources and tutorials to help you get started and make the most of your advertising efforts, even if you're fairly novice.

Facebook Ads enables you to reach a vast audience, including users who may not actively search for your services but could be interested based on their demographics, interests, and behaviour. With its various ad formats and placements, such as News Feed, Stories, and Marketplace, Facebook Ads provides a versatile platform for promoting your aesthetics practice.

The paid channels with the highest ROI are
Facebook and Google Search advertising.

HTTPS://WWW.HUBSPOT.COM/MARKETING-STATISTICS

LinkedIn is a powerful online advertising service for the LinkedIn platform; it's really for businesses looking to target professionals and decision-makers. LinkedIn offers a unique opportunity to reach a more niche audience interested in your aesthetics services:

- **Professional audience:** LinkedIn's user base consists primarily of professionals and decision-makers, making it an excellent platform for targeting potential clients in specific high-end industries or job roles.
- **Precise targeting options:** LinkedIn Ads offers detailed targeting options based on job title, company size, industry, and more, so if you want to be the aesthetician to lawyers (and there's no reason that's a stupid idea), you can focus your advertising efforts on precisely that audience.
- **Lead generation:** With LinkedIn's lead generation forms, you can collect valuable information from potential clients who express interest in your practice, streamlining the process of converting leads to customers.
- **Usability and Software:** LinkedIn Campaign Manager is the platform's advertising management tool, providing an intuitive interface for creating, managing, and optimising ad campaigns.

While LinkedIn's user base is smaller than that of Google and Facebook, its professional focus makes it an ideal platform for targeting a more specific audience. LinkedIn Ads offers various ad formats, including sponsored content, sponsored InMail, and display ads, giving you plenty of flexibility.

Twitter Ads is the online advertising platform that allows you to promote your products and services to...wait for it...Twitter's vast user base. With its real-time nature and emphasis on trending topics, Twitter offers a unique opportunity for businesses to engage with potential clients in a more conversational way. Twitter's got a bit of a bad reputation at the moment, but there's no reason for a small business to get tarred with the same brush, and if anything, it'll mean that the rates you have to pay may be reduced. Twitter offers:

- **Real-time engagement:** Twitter's real-time nature allows you to engage with potential clients as they interact with trending topics or relevant hashtags, increasing the chances of capturing their attention.

- **Advanced targeting options:** Like all the other platforms, Twitter Ads offers a range of targeting options based on demographics, interests, and behaviour; but it has something of an advantage thanks to the heavily refined and real-time nature of the content on the platform.

- **Promoted tweets and accounts:** With Twitter Ads, you can promote specific tweets or your entire account, increasing visibility and attracting more clients.

- **Usability and Software:** Twitter Ads uses a service called Twitter Ads Manager, a simple and user-friendly interface for creating and managing ad campaigns. Again, beware: there are recent stories of Twitter underinvesting in its platform, and advertisers finding problems.

Twitter's user base may not be as large as Facebook or Google, but its unique, real-time nature provides a valuable platform for engaging with potential clients in a timely and relevant manner. Twitter Ads offers various ad formats, such as promoted tweets, promoted accounts, and promoted trends, allowing you to tailor your advertising approach to user themes.

Pinterest Ads? Wait, what? Yep. Pinterest Ads, also known as Promoted Pins, are designed for businesses looking to reach users in a visually driven environment – and aesthetics practitioners certainly fit that description. As a platform centred around images and inspiration, Pinterest can be an excellent choice for aesthetics practices looking to inspire potential clients with visually appealing content:

- **Visual focus:** Pinterest's image-centric platform allows you to showcase your aesthetics services through high-quality visuals, making it easier to capture the attention of potential clients.

- **Targeting options:** Pinterest Ads offers targeting options based on demographics, interests, and keywords, enabling you to reach the most relevant audience.
- **High purchase intent:** Pinterest users often visit the platform for inspiration and ideas, making them likely to be further along the buying process, ready to engage with and consider purchasing your aesthetics services.
- **Just not #1:** Since Pinterest is rarely anyone's #1 go-to for advertising, it's likely to cost less to get started.
- **Usability and Software:** Pinterest Ads are managed through the Pinterest Ads Manager, which offers all the tools you need for creating, managing, and optimising ad campaigns.

While Pinterest's user base is smaller than some of the other platforms mentioned, its visual nature and high purchase intent make it a valuable platform for aesthetics practices. Pinterest Ads formats include standard pins, video pins and carousel pins, providing flexibility in how you present your services to potential clients.

YOUR ADVERTISING STRATEGY

This sounds like it's going to be complicated, but it doesn't have to be. It's fundamentally about having a plan and minimising any waste of money. Before you begin planning your online advertising spend, set some clear goals and Key Performance Indicators (KPIs – the numbers) to guide your efforts. Typically, you'll want to increase website traffic, generating leads, or boosting sales of specific products and treatments. Above all, note right now that those are not the same thing! For example, people often buy relatively inexpensive products on a whim. They don't buy expensive invasive treatments instantly, though – that sort of thing will usually require more touchpoints and more expense.

Similarly, select the KPIs that will help you track progress towards those goals. Typically, you'll want to monitor click-through rates (CTRs – who has clicked through to your website), cost per click (CPC – how much those clicks cost, particularly in the highly competitive world of pay-per-click advertising), conversion rates (how many clicks turn into actual purchases), or return on ad spend (ROAS – overall income for money spent). By setting specific, measurable targets for your KPIs, you'll be able to evaluate the success of your campaigns and make informed adjustments as needed.

With so many online advertising platforms available, it's important to choose the ones that will best serve your goals. Consider the following when selecting platforms (we look at them in more detail in the section above):

- **Demographics:** Research the user demographics of each platform to ensure they align with your target audience. For aesthetics practices, platforms like Facebook, Instagram, and Pinterest, which have a strong focus on visuals and cater to a wide age range, may be ideal.
- **Ad formats:** Each platform offers different ad formats, such as image, video, or carousel ads. Choose platforms that support the formats you think will be most effective for showcasing your treatments and engaging your audience.
- And of course, **cost:** Compare the advertising costs of different platforms and consider your budget when making your selection.

Despite all these considerations, the performance of platforms will change over time, and you will usually find that more than one platform is worth your effort (typically Google for breadth plus one more for laser-sharp targeting).

When you're ready to roll, it's time to create some ads. Your ad content should capture the attention of your target audience and inspire them to take action. Keep these tips in mind:

- **Use high-quality visuals:** Aesthetics is a visually driven industry, so invest in professional photography or design services to create eye-catching images or videos that showcase your treatments and results. If you've read the sections above, you'll know that design doesn't have to cost a fortune, but investing in an attractive visual narrative is worth its weight in gold.
- **Craft a clear message:** Keep your ad copy concise and focused on the benefits of your treatments, addressing your audience's needs and desires. Include a clear call-to-action (CTA) that encourages viewers to learn more, book a consultation, or make a purchase.
- **Be authentic:** Represent your brand and practice authentically, showcasing your unique selling points, expertise and the people who make things tick.

To maximize the effectiveness of your ads, you'll want to continuously test and optimize them. Use A/B testing (see email marketing, chapter 6 above) to compare different ad elements, such as headlines, images, or CTAs, and work out which versions perform best. Monitor those KPIs and other campaign performance metrics closely to keep improving your results. Factors to consider when optimizing your ads include:

- **Targeting:** Refine your audience targeting based on performance data. You may find that certain demographics or interests respond better to your ads, allowing you to focus your efforts on the most receptive audience segments.
- **Ad scheduling:** Analyze your ad performance by time of day or day of the week to identify optimal times for running your ads. This can help you allocate your budget more effectively and potentially reduce your overall costs.
- **Bid adjustments:** Experiment with different bidding strategies to find the most cost-effective approach for your campaigns. Monitor your

CPC, CTR, and conversion rates to ensure you're achieving the best possible results for your budget.

As a matter of course, note that you can always target more effectively, and you can always waste more time working out targeting strategies. There will be an optimum effort which gives you the right amount of efficiency for the right amount of time spent on getting your targeting right.

All that targeting effort is about optimising your spend – getting the biggest bang for your budgetary buck. Here are some more tips to help you optimize your ad spend:

- **Set a budget:** Establish an overall advertising budget, as well as individual budgets for each platform or campaign. This will help you allocate resources strategically and ensure you're not overspending on any one aspect of your advertising strategy.
- **Keep an eye on the KPIs:** Regularly review your campaign performance, tracking your KPIs and ROI (Return On Investment). Never be scared to reallocate your budget to more effective channels.
- **Use automated bidding tools:** Many advertising platforms offer automated bidding tools that can help you optimize your ad spend by adjusting bids based on real-time data. These tools will help you achieve your desired KPIs more efficiently and often at a lower cost.
- **Optimize for conversions:** When setting up your campaigns, focus on optimizing for conversions, such as booking consultations or completing a purchase, rather than simply driving clicks or impressions. This will ensure that your investment turns into hard cash.
- **Be proactive:** Be prepared to adjust your budgets based on campaign performance and any changes in your marketing goals or priorities. This may involve increasing your budget for high-performing campaigns or reducing spend on underperforming ads.

By following these guidelines and continually refining your online advertising strategy, you'll be well on your way to creating a successful campaign strategy that drives results for your aesthetics practice. Remember that advertising is an ongoing process, so stay flexible, go with the data, and be prepared to make adjustments as needed to ensure you're making the most of your budget.

RETARGETING

There's one more aspect of online advertising you should get to grips with: 'retargeting'. Retargeting is an effective way to re-engage potential clients who have previously interacted with your website or ads. By showing ads to these individuals as they browse other websites or social media platforms, you can keep your practice top of mind and increase the likelihood of them converting into clients.

Customers are up to 70% more likely to buy your product when you use retargeting.

HTTPS://TECHJURY.NET/BLOG/PPC-STATS/#GREF

Retargeting will require you to implement tracking pixels or tags on your website to collect data on user behaviour and allow retargeting to happen. More than for generic advertising, it's worth segmenting a retargeting audience into e.g. those who viewed a specific treatment page, added an item to a shopping cart, or submitted a contact form. The fact that they have been on your website gives you an important and useful parameter with which to target them with future creative.

And then, of course, create personalized ads for each audience segment, addressing their specific interests or concerns, and offering an incentive to return to your website and complete their purchase.

Retargeting is a little more complex but can be particularly useful for drawing back people who were on the very cusp of making a purchase.

DIGGING DOWN INTO THE NUMBERS

Above, we've had a look at some of the key metrics in online advertising. For most campaigns, they will do just fine. But while CPC, CTR, and ROAS are important metrics, there are several other lesser-known metrics that can provide valuable insights into your advertising performance – deploy them as you see fit!:

- **Impressions:** The number of times your ad is displayed. This helps you understand the reach of your campaigns and can be an indicator of brand awareness. Low impressions with high response suggest that you're hitting the mark with your customers; a huge number of impressions with a low response means you should probably reinvestigate your creative approach.
- **View-through rate (VTR):** The percentage of users who watch your video ads for a certain duration (e.g., 25%, 50%, 75%, or 100%). This metric evaluates the engagement and effectiveness of video ads.
- **Cost per acquisition (CPA):** The average cost of acquiring a customer through your ads. This metric can help you determine the cost-effectiveness of your campaigns and identify areas for improvement. If the CPA is more than your planned marketing budget, or the profit you'd make on a procedure with the client, then you're effectively losing money.
- **Conversion rate (CVR):** The percentage of users who take a desired action (e.g., booking a consultation or making a purchase) after clicking on your ad. This metric is crucial for assessing the effectiveness of your ads in driving ongoing activity. Increase your CVR and you're increasing your profitability.

- **Lifetime value (LTV):** A very subtle and useful metric: this is the esti-mated net profit attributed to the entire future relationship with a customer. Understanding LTV can help you make informed decisions about your ad spend and customer acquisition strategy, because if the average client stays with you for 12 treatments, say, then they are worth twice as much marketing effort (and spend) as a client who only stays for six treatments.
- **Bounce rate:** The percentage of users who visit your website after clicking on your ad but leave without taking any action. A high bounce rate may indicate that your ad or landing page is not effec-tively engaging users or meeting their expectations.

To effectively interpret and use these ad spend statistics, monitor your ad spend and performance metrics on a regular basis to identify trends, areas of success, and opportunities for improvement. Then make some comparisons. Analyze your ad spend and performance data across different advertising platforms to determine which channels are deliv-ering the best ROI. Similarly, compare your performance to industry benchmarks or historical data to see if you're broadly performing to expectations.

Look for correlations between ad spend and key performance met-rics, such as conversions or LTV, to help you understand the relationship between your advertising investment and business outcomes.

To monitor your overall advertising ROI (shorthand for: am I smashing the ball out of the park or losing money hand over fist?):

- **Set up tracking everywhere you can:** Implement tracking tools and pixels on your website and advertising platforms to collect accurate data on user behaviour, conversions, and revenue.
- **Establish a reporting process:** Create a process for regularly review-ing your advertising performance and ROI, including setting up custom reports or dashboards that display key metrics and insights.

Come back to these every week for the first few weeks, then every month thereafter.

- **Calculate ROI for individual campaigns and platforms:** Determine the ROI for each campaign and advertising platform by comparing revenue generated to ad spend. This will help you identify the most profitable channels and allocate your budget accordingly.
- **Factor in the long-term value:** Consider the long-term value of your advertising efforts, such as increased brand awareness, customer loyalty, and repeat business.
- **Keep optimizing:** Continuously test and optimize your campaigns, using the ROI data to inform your decisions. This may involve adjusting targeting, ad creative, bidding strategies, or platform allocations to improve your overall performance.

CHECKLIST

☑ Set clear goals and Key Performance Indicators (KPIs) to guide your advertising efforts.

☑ Choose the right advertising platforms based on demographics, ad formats, and cost.

☑ Explore the various ad formats and types available on each platform to decide how you want to present your practice to potential clients.

☑ Pay attention to the unique features of each platform, such as real-time engagement on Twitter.

☑ Don't overlook lesser-used platforms like Pinterest Ads, which may offer lower costs and less competition.

☑ Create compelling ads with high-quality visuals, clear messaging, and authentic representation.

☑ Refine audience targeting, ad scheduling, and bidding strategies to improve campaign performance.

☑ Implement retargeting to re-engage potential clients who have previously interacted with your website or ads.

☑ Continuously test and optimize your ads using A/B testing and analyze your ad spend and performance data across platforms and compare them to industry benchmarks or historical data.

LOCAL SEO AND LOCAL MARKETING

In today's fast-paced digital world, one of the most effective ways to achieve engagement with your audience is by harnessing the power of local SEO (search engine optimization) and local marketing tactics. Most of your clients will be in your local area, so let's put some effort into reaching them!

Local SEO is the process of optimizing your online presence to attract more business from relevant local searches. These searches typically take place on search engines like Google and Bing, or local listings sites like Yelp and TripAdvisor. Local SEO is essential for aesthetics clinics as it enables you to target potential clients within your specific geographical area, ensuring that their services are easily discoverable by those who need them the most. Local SEO will give you:

- **Increased visibility:** making your clinic more visible to people searching for aesthetic treatments in your area. It helps you rank higher in search engine results pages (SERPs), allowing you to capture the attention of potential clients.
- **Better credibility:** A strong online presence that features positive reviews, accurate information, and engaging content can boost your clinic's credibility. This, in turn, will build trust among potential clients, increasing the likelihood that they will choose your clinic over your competitors.

- **Improved website traffic:** By optimizing your website for local searches, you are more likely to attract visitors who are genuinely interested in your services. This can lead to higher conversion rates, as potential clients are more likely to take action, such as booking a consultation or making an inquiry.
- **Competitive advantage:** Local SEO can help you stay ahead of your competitors by ensuring that your clinic appears prominently in local searches. This is especially important in a crowded market.

Google still accounts for well over 90% (https://gs.statcounter.com/search-engine-market-share) of web searches. A study conducted in 2020 found that 46% (https://blog.hubspot.com/marketing/local-seo-stats) of all Google searches have a local intent, meaning that users are looking for products, services, or information specific to their geographic area.

So, here are some of the key strategies for boosting your clinic's local SEO efforts:

- **Local Listings and Directories:** Claiming and optimizing your clinic's local listings on various platforms is essential for improving your online visibility. Start by creating and optimizing your Google My Business (GMB) listing. This is a powerful tool that helps you manage your online presence across Google, including Search and Maps. Ensure that your clinic's name, address, phone number, and other relevant information are accurate and always kept up to date. We'll look at GMB in the next section, but don't stop there: also claim and optimize your listings on other local directories, such as Yelp, TripAdvisor, and any industry-specific directories. These platforms not only improve your online presence but also offer an opportunity for clients to leave reviews, which can boost your credibility.

- This brings us to **Reviews and Ratings:** Reviews play a significant role in local SEO, as they don't just affect potential clients' perceptions; they also influence how search engines rank your clinic! Encourage satisfied clients to leave reviews on platforms like Google, Yelp, and Facebook. Respond to both positive and negative reviews professionally and promptly, showing potential clients that you care about their feedback and are committed to providing top-notch service.

- **Local Content and Keywords:** Creating content that targets local keywords can help search engines understand the geographical relevance of your clinic. For instance, you might create blog posts about popular aesthetic treatments in your area, or share news and updates about local events your clinic is involved in. Include local keywords (especially town/city names) in your content, meta tags, and image "alt" tags to further optimize your website for local search. Meta and alt tags, by the way, are bits of information which are not (usually) shown to the user – that makes them a great place to hide location information which you might not usually find a place for in your text.

- **Local Link Building:** We saw above in Chapter 3 (your website) that backlinks – links to your site from other websites – are of high search value. Acquiring links from reputable local websites (e.g. local newspapers, directories, blogs, etc.) can improve your clinic's online credibility and search rankings. Reach out to local news outlets, bloggers, and industry influencers to feature your clinic or collaborate on content. By building these strong relationships within your community, you can establish your clinic as a trusted source of information and expertise.

- **Social Media and Local Engagement:** Leveraging social media platforms like Facebook, Instagram, Twitter and Nextdoor can help you engage with your local audience and promote your aesthetic clinic. Share updates about your services, special offers, and local events to connect with potential clients and showcase your clinic's involvement in the community. You can also use social media to gather reviews and engage with clients, which can further enhance your local SEO efforts. Local is an extraordinary hotbed of grassroots marketing opportunities – you can be sure that there are multiple local Facebook groups and even WhatsApp groups to get involved with.

As always, it's important to regularly assess your performance and identify new opportunities for growth. Monitor your online presence, track your search rankings, and analyze your website traffic to understand the impact of your local SEO strategies.

Keep an eye on your competitors and stay informed about local trends to identify gaps in the market and seize opportunities as they arise. By staying proactive and adapting to the ever-changing landscape, you can ensure that your aesthetic clinic remains a top choice for local clients.

GO FOR GOLD WITH GOOGLE MY BUSINESS

Above, we mentioned the importance of Google My Business (GMB) as a marketing channel. In this section, we'll help you use it to increase visibility and engagement with potential clients in your local area.

The number of searches containing "near me" has increased by more than 200% over the last two years, according to Google's Consumer Insights.

(BB DIGITAL GOOGLE OPTIMISATION COURSE)

Google My Business (GMB) is a free, easy-to-use tool that enables you to manage your online presence across Google, including Search and Maps. By verifying and editing your business information, you can help customers find you, provide them with accurate details, and showcase your practice's unique selling points.

I obsess over GMB because it's where potential patients for most aesthetics clinics, within the right catchment area, go to find a clinic at the moment when they are at their "highest point of intent". By that, I mean they are ready to go; they've decided that they either have a condition that they would like to resolve, or an aesthetic concern that they would like to improve, and they are ready to do something about it. If your clinic is not there when they make that search, then no amount of website elegance is going to help; they'll end up with one of your competitors instead.

Your Google Business Profile is therefore also not something that you can leave to be created automatically (by reviews, public records and circumstance). And it is not something that you should consider to be "fire and forget". It should become part of your weekly, monthly and quarterly marketing plans (and the good news is, it doesn't have to be a huge sap on your time).

In short, I believe very strongly that putting effort into Google Local is the most effective model for attracting new patients to your clinic, and then using social media (see the next chapter) to engage them both as they progress through their consideration process and once they become a patient, to ensure you remain front of mind.

This rebalancing of focus onto Google Local, ironically, tends to lead to you having a higher quality follower list on e.g. your Instagram page too, because it will fill up with people who have high intent, live within 20 miles of your practice, or have already become a patient and no doubt have great things to say about you! This is much better than having a larger number of followers who don't live anywhere near you, have no intention of booking in to see you, or – worst of all – are actually just competitors.

I've already used different terms here, and we should take a moment to examine them. GMB is a business listing (very much like the Yellow Pages, for any older readers…). This information is used for Google "Near Me" searches which appear on Google search results and in the Google Maps app. Together, this is the Google Local architecture.

Crucially, these search results will appear next to, or beneath, a map. And on the first page of Google (this is even more important on smartphones), only three results are typically shown; so it's a very competitive piece of screen real estate, but the rewards are great: over 70% of all traffic for a search term is taken by those top three results in that map pack. The work required to establish a strong Google Local presence starts with your Google Business Profile.

Follow these steps to optimize your GMB listing and attract more clients:

- First up, **claim and verify your listing:** To start, you'll need to create or claim your GMB listing. Visit the Google My Business website and sign in with your Google account. You can then either claim your business profile, if it already exists, or add your business if it doesn't. Enter your business name, address, and phone number, and select the appropriate business category. If your business already exists in Google's database, you can claim it to start making changes. Google will send you a verification code via postcard, email, or phone to confirm that you're the legitimate owner of the business. Once set up:

  - ☐ Verify your listing
  - ☐ Include relevant keywords
  - ☐ Make sure you've added your website link (imagine customers getting all the way to your listing and then not being able to click through!)
  - ☐ Add your opening hours and remember to update them if they change seasonally or during holidays. This is a surprisingly good source of "on a whim" visits.
  - ☐ Add the address and place a map marker
  - ☐ Add an area code to the phone number

- **Use Google "Justifications".** 65% of Google searches do not generate a click. It's as competitive as any other type of search marketing:

you need to be able to stand out and differentiate in your listing. An excellent way to stand out is to highlight your offer through the justifications feature, which is why over half of local search results include justifications. These are text excerpts that appear to customers in the Local Pack or on Google Maps, additional information about the establishment's offering that justify (literally) its presence in the results according to Google's thinking. Justifications come from several sources:

- ☐ Your website – a little 'globe' icon in your listing shows that Google has connected content from your website to the term which the user has just searched for.
- ☐ Reviews – a little 'person' icon tells the user that Google has found high-value information, relevant to the user's search in a patient review.
- ☐ Services – a blue tick (nothing to do with Twitter!) means that Google has tied the user's search directly to a service you have listed in your Google My Business profile.
- ☐ Google Posts – an exclamation mark similarly ties content from a Google Post to the search made by the user.

This is Google directly showing us how it ranks clinics from top to bottom of individual results. The more "justifications" you can impact, the greater the chance you have of achieving top ranking among relevant searches.

- ■ **Provide and maintain accurate information:** Ensure your business name, address, phone number, and website are accurate and consistent across all online platforms, including your website and social media channels. Consistency is crucial for search engines to recognize your business and improve your rankings in local search results.
- ■ **Choose relevant categories:** Google allows you to select primary and secondary categories for your aesthetics practice. The primary

category should best describe your core offering (e.g., "Aesthetic Clinic" or "Medical Spa"), while secondary categories can represent additional services or specializations (e.g., "Laser Hair Removal Service" or "Skin Care Clinic"). Accurate categorization helps Google understand your business better and rank you higher for relevant search queries.

- **Write a compelling business description:** Your GMB listing features a description field that allows you to provide more information about your aesthetics practice. Use this space very carefully to highlight what makes your business unique and why potential clients should choose you. Keep it concise, engaging, and informative, and avoid any promotional or salesy language.

- **Add high-quality photos and videos:** Visual content plays a major role in attracting potential clients. Upload high-resolution images and videos that showcase your facilities, treatments, and results. Consider including staff headshots and images of the equipment or products you use. Regularly (we recommend quarterly) update your visual content to keep it fresh and engaging.

- **Enable and manage reviews:** Google reviews are a crucial factor in your local SEO performance. Encourage satisfied clients to leave positive reviews and make time to respond to all reviews, whether they are positive or negative. And you will, no matter how hard you try, receive the odd negative review. Relax – everyone does. Take it as an opportunity to engage, learn and ultimately rescue the situation. By engaging with your reviewers, you show that you value their feedback and are committed to providing the best service.

- **Deploy Google Posts:** I briefly mentioned Google Posts above. They allow you to share updates, promotions, and events directly on your GMB listing. Regularly post engaging content that showcases your latest treatments, special offers, or upcoming events. Google Posts can help keep your listing fresh and relevant, increasing the likelihood of potential clients engaging with your practice. And Google Posts don't have to mean new effort – simply include Google Posts occasionally as part of your social media activity.

- **Learn with GMB Insights:** Like all platforms, there are stats to learn from. Google My Business provides insights into how customers find and interact with your listing. Monitor these metrics to understand the effectiveness of your listings. For instance, you can track the number of views your listing gets, the types of actions users take (calling, visiting your website, or requesting directions), and where your listing appears in search results. This data will help you to make informed decisions about your local marketing strategies and further optimize your GMB listing.

- **Optimize for mobile users:** More and more people are searching for businesses on their mobile devices. Make sure your GMB listing and website are mobile-friendly (most of this will be done automatically) to provide a seamless experience for potential clients. This includes having a responsive website design, fast-loading pages, and easy-to-navigate menus.

- **Add services and pricing:** Your GMB listing allows you to include a list of the services you offer and their respective prices. Providing this information can help potential clients understand your offerings and make informed decisions about choosing your aesthetics practice. Make sure to keep this information up to date and consider including any special packages or promotions you may be running. However, especially if you're a high-end business, you may prefer not to show prices: you will turn away very price-sensitive customers. There's no right answer here – it really does depend on your clientele.

- **Use the Questions & Answers feature:** Google My Business has a Q&A section where potential clients can ask questions about your aesthetics practice. You should check this section regularly and provide accurate answers to any inquiries. This not only demonstrates your expertise but also helps build trust with potential clients. You might also encourage your existing customers to contribute to the

Q&A section, as their first-hand experiences can be valuable to pro-spective clients.

- **One click to appointment booking:** If your practice offers online appointment booking, enable this feature on your GMB listing. This allows potential clients to book appointments directly from your listing, making it super convenient for them and improving your conversion rates.

In short, optimizing your Google My Business listing is a crucial step in your local marketing efforts. It's easy, logical, and embedded on one plat-form. And you can follow the above ideas in pretty much any order – you don't have to do it all at once. What's not to love?

ADVANCED GOOGLE MY BUSINESS

I said earlier that I am obsessive about local listings and GMB, so I'd like to give you a little Black Belt insight into advanced GMB success. You've probably read the section above, and I hope you've at least claimed your listing and begun to add basic information like opening times.

But I also mentioned (under "Justifications" above) that Google uses an intricate set of carefully hidden "ranking factors" to decide who appears on the top-3 list of every search. There are actually over 70 rank-ing factors, but don't panic – we're not going to game the system on all of them! I think there are eleven which can really move the needle on your local business success. Here goes!

- **Proximity.** The core principle of Google Local is that it shows the customer businesses which are near to them. It stands to reason, therefore, that the closer your clinic address is to the centre of your town or city, the more times your profile will show up in generic search results (e.g. "Skin tightening, Liverpool"). But for local searches, potential customers will see you in different positions in the results according to how close your clinic is to their exact location. Clients often tell me confidently that they are always #1 for dermal fillers on local searches – when they ran the search in their premises! Use tools like BrightLocal to see realistically where your business ranks for local performance. Then, as well as having the correct address listed and popping a map marker into Google Maps, tick these three off your list:

- ☐ Ensure your town or city appears in the metadata on your website
- ☐ Ensure it also appears regularly (but comfortably) in your content
- ☐ Ensure your location is verified in GBP

■ **Reviews.** I cover reviews properly later (see "Managing your Online Reputation"), but note that after proximity, the amount of positive reviews on your Google profile is the next most decisive factor in determining the success of your listing. If your patients are kind enough to mention the name of the treatment they have purchased and your location too, then so much the better!

■ **Content.** We discussed content above. Google has always rated providers of high-quality content above other options, and that's also true in Local. Check out the content advice in "Content Marketing" above, ensure a steady but manageable flow of new material to your website, and try to post Google Posts every week (these can be based on your blogs or other material, so they don't need to be dramatically new).

■ **Activity.** Update your GMB profile regularly – twice a week is ideal. New photos, videos, posts, replies to reviews, new Questions and Answers, and edits and updates to your Services section all count.

■ **Your Website.** Google scans your website and its contents before your profile is placed in search results and rescans it regularly. This is how Google can add the blue globe icon to searches where your website includes terms which the user has searched for; signifying increased relevance (see "Justifications" above). Make sure your website includes appropriate search terms (see "Your Website" above). Include relevant local meta tags, titles on your website pages and schema code references (if this sounds like wizardry, ask your friendly local web expert). Embed your Google Map on your website (this is easy – it's one line of code).

- **Citations.** Citations are listings in reputable online references to your business that feature its name, address, and phone number (NAP). Having your business listed in trusted online directories sends signals to Google that improves its degree of certainty that your business exists and is credible. The more listings in online directories, the better. The nice folks at BrightLocal automate this process, so check them out. Also, broker links with other local websites (your local Chamber of Commerce or association is a good place to start). And make sure your NAP is consistent everywhere – if you change contact details, put effort into keeping these external sources updated!

- **Services.** If you have chosen the correct kind of category for your profile (usually 'Skincare Clinic', then your Google Business Profile may also offer an option to add the services that you provide, along with their descriptions. If your business has multiple categories, group services together into sections under the appropriate category to keep your services organised. Clearly, maintaining this list is dynamite for accurate listing, so fully populate your services list, duplicating them if appropriate for each skin condition you treat. Add descriptions and pricing if you can, and review listings regularly.

- **Photos.** The photo section is one of the most overlooked features of Google Business Profiles, but it's powerful stuff. Businesses with GMB photos receive 42% more driving directions requests and 35% more click-throughs to their website than more anonymous competitors! Photos build trust and remove questions – they give customers a sense of the quality of your operation. So, ensure images are always high quality. Showcase you and your team. With permission, share those all-important 'before & afters'. And use keywords when naming photos, so that Google knows exactly what to show and when.

- **Q&A/FAQ.** In June 2021, Google rolled out a new function elevating the importance of Q&As (the ability for potential customers to ask questions about your business from within the Google interface). This means two things. Firstly, like all other marketing activity, you need to devote a little time to the Q&A function. Encourage questions, answer them in detail (including keywords, of course) and aim for 20+ questions in your listing. Secondly, reap the rewards: snippets of Q&As that feature keywords directly relevant to a user's search will now appear in search results, upping your profile and your reputation within those search fields. The more key questions and answers your business profile features, the more chance you have of ranking top for the search terms that will bring you new patients.

- **Social Media.** Yes, Google checks everything. I mentioned at the top of this section that Social Media is a big part of your Google Local strategy, and that's because your social media impacts your Google local results. These factors change constantly but include the number of times your business is mentioned in social media, the number of reviews on your social media pages, the longevity of your Facebook or Instagram pages, completed and optimised biographies on social media (all to show that you're for real) and consistent NAP information – again.

- **Metrics and behaviour.** Finally, we need to note something at the heart of the way Google thinks. It loves metrics, so what people do when they see your GMB profile is important. If, for whatever reason, they run a mile, Google will notice. It uses propensity to click, time spent on the page, click-to-call usage from mobile phones and bounce rate, among others, to decide whether to continue to list you high or not. This is all part of Google's desire to optimise for relevance to searchers; so, whilst you can't change the system, you can recognise it and ensure that with high-quality content, your listing frequency is amplified rather than being penalised.

MORE LOCAL MARKETING TACTICS

You've probably guessed that I'm a huge fan of the Google My Business listing. Local marketing works because it cuts out 90% of the competition before you even start. If you're in Walsall, the cost of targeting people in Walsall is a lot less than targeting the whole country, and with a much higher conversion rate.

In this spirit, there are many other local marketing tactics that you can employ to effectively market your practice in your local area. By maintaining consistency in your marketing activities and keeping a constant drumbeat of good ideas, good news, and positive perceptions, you can set yourself apart from the competition and build lasting relationships with your clients.

Don't try these without a strong online presence first (see Chapter 3, Your Website, and Chapter 9, Social Media, if these are not looking too good yet!), as your website is still going to be the first place people go to check your business out, once they have had an initial contact with you on the basis of these local marketing themes. Ready to go? Here are some ideas you might like to try:

- **Engage with local community events:** Participate in community events, such as charity fundraisers, local festivals, or health and wellness fairs. These events provide opportunities to network, increase brand awareness, and demonstrate your commitment to the local community. Consider offering free consultations, demonstrations, or samples of your services to showcase your expertise and attract potential clients.
- **Develop partnerships with local businesses:** Collaborate with complementary businesses in your area, such as fitness centres, beauty

salons, or wellness clinics. Cross-promotions, joint events, or referral programs can help expand your reach and introduce your practice to new clients. Ensure these partnerships align with your brand values and target audience.

- **Offer exclusive local promotions:** Attract new clients and reward loyal ones by offering promotions or discounts exclusive to your local community. This might include a loyalty programme that rewards regular – but local – customers. Promote these offers through your website, social media channels, and email marketing.

- **Use local media:** Reach out to local newspapers, magazines, radio stations, or bloggers for coverage of your aesthetics practice. Share stories about your practice, such as new treatments or technologies, client success stories, and particularly community involvement. If you choose to advertise with these outlets, all of them will entertain the idea of adding editorial (or advertorial) footage to any financial commitment to advertising.

- **Encourage word-of-mouth referrals:** Word-of-mouth marketing is The. Best. Way. to attract new clients. Encourage happy clients to share their experiences with friends and family. You could offer incentives, such as a referral discount or a free treatment, to motivate clients to spread the word about your practice, particularly on review sites.

- **Collect and showcase testimonials:** We cover this above (Chapter 6, Social Media) – for now, let's just say that since most customers are local, local testimonials are particularly valuable.

- **Leverage local influencers:** Partner with local influencers or bloggers who share your target audience and have a strong presence on social media. Influencers can help promote your practice, review your services, or share their experiences with their followers, resulting in increased brand awareness and new clients.

- **Conduct workshops or seminars:** Host educational workshops or seminars to educate your local community about the benefits of your aesthetic treatments, share your expertise, and showcase your practice. These events can help position you as a thought leader and build relationships without being too salesy.

- ■ **Focus on building a local network:** Attend local business events, Chamber of Commerce meetings, or industry-specific conferences to expand your network and build relationships with other professionals in your area. Networking can lead to potential partnerships, referrals, and increased visibility for your practice.

In all of these activities, there are a couple of universal pieces of advice. First, consistency in your branding and messaging across all marketing channels is crucial for building recognition and trust. Ensure your logo, colour schemes and tone of voice are uniform across your website, social media, advertising, and printed materials. And make sure they all match you – the person fronting the whole operation to your local area and the customers in it.

Second, all of this falls apart if you don't provide exceptional customer service. A genuinely excellent offer is what will allow you to build long-term relationships and encourage customers to refer their friends and family to your practice. Your local community is core to your profitability, and bad news travels very fast indeed. Train your staff to be knowledgeable, attentive, and responsive to client needs. Always listen to feedback and put the client's experience first.

CHECKLIST

☑ Claim and optimize local listings and keep them up-to-date.

☑ Encourage and respond to reviews.

☑ Use local content and keywords to optimize your website for local search.

☑ Build local backlinks, e.g. newspapers, directories, and blogs.

☑ Engage with the local community on social media platforms like Facebook, Instagram, Twitter, and Nextdoor.

☑ Use all the Google My Business features – services and pricing, the Q&A section, one-click appointments, etc.

☑ Engage with local community events to increase brand awareness and connect with potential clients.

☑ Encourage word-of-mouth referrals and incentivize clients to share their positive experiences.

☑ Workshops and seminars can also be great for building relationships in your local area.

SOCIAL MEDIA MARKETING

Social media marketing is a bit of a minefield. In today's digital age, social media plays an increasingly important role in the marketing strategies of aesthetics practices. The right platforms can help you build brand awareness, engage with potential clients, and showcase your services effectively.

86% of Women Use Social Media for Purchasing Advice.

HTTPS://DIGITALMARKETINGINSTITUTE.COM/BLOG/20-INFLUENCER-MARKETING-STATISTICS-THAT-WILL-SURPRISE-YOU

Do bear in mind though, that there are a good number of aesthetic clinics that run perfectly well without social media in their lives – just as there are plenty of people who cope without it. Some practitioners thrive just because of their location (especially if you're the only game in town). Others are just happy with a lifestyle business that works on word-of-mouth referral. So, you don't have to operate on social media, and I say that because it can be daunting, eat up time, and be incredibly fast-changing. I advise that if you are looking to scale your practice, and if you serve patients aged between 25 and 55, then social media should at least be somewhere on your agenda.

CHOOSING THE RIGHT PLATFORMS

Social media is way more than just Instagram, although 'Insta' has exploded among aestheticians because of its visual focus (we'll look at this in more detail below). In this section, we will discuss the process of selecting the most suitable social media platforms for your clinic.

Again, I have to add a caveat: there is no single answer here, because social media moves so fast – platforms have a habit of falling in and out of favour with various generations. I personally know of practices that have scaled purely thanks to building a committed audience on YouTube. I have also coached a practitioner who gets great results from posting content on Pinterest boards. I know doctors who are creating stunning results on TikTok. And I have even dealt with a clinic in Australia whose very successful strategy has been built on posting a mountain of content on Reddit – this surprising approach generates a steady stream of enquiries every week! All of these practices are putting in the hard yards and getting the results.

In Chapter 2, we looked at target audiences. Given that there is such a plethora of social media services today, it will make sense to start where your audience is. Over-50s, for example, are a big segment for aesthetics practitioners – but very few of them are on TikTok! Remembering the basics of your target audience will help you make informed decisions about which platforms are most likely to connect with them.

Here are some of the leading options:

- **Facebook:** With its wide reach and diverse user base, Facebook is a valuable platform for reaching a broad audience. Facebook Pages and Groups can help you build a community around your clinic, while super-targeted advertising allows you to reach potential clients in your area.
- **Instagram:** As a visually-oriented platform, Instagram is ideal for showcasing images (before-and-after, premises, events, etc.),

behind-the-scenes stories, and short videos of your aesthetic treatments. With its younger user base, Instagram is particularly well-suited to targeting millennials and Gen Z, but it has a remarkably broad age range of users in general. "Insta" is also fast to create content for.

- **Twitter:** Twitter's fast-paced, conversational nature makes it a great platform for engaging with clients. However, the platform's character limit and basic handling of pictures and videos can make it challenging to share in-depth content or showcase visual elements of your treatments. Good for quick nuggets!

- **TikTok:** Wow. What can we say about the meteoric rise of TikTok? However, it's adored by younger audiences but may also ultimately be subject to wide-ranging restrictions due to fears of data leaks by its Chinese owners. A platform for short, highly creative videos, you can use TikTok to share engaging, informative content about treatments and skincare routines. Go big on showcasing your clinic's personality.

- **Pinterest:** A highly visual platform, Pinterest allows users to save and share images and ideas that inspire them. For aesthetics clinics, Pinterest can be an excellent place to share images, treatment ideas, advice and product reviews with a predominantly female audience. It's rarely the first place to invest in social, but some businesses find it to be a remarkably effective slow burn.

- **LinkedIn:** The global professional networking site, LinkedIn can help you build connections with industry peers and showcase your expertise through articles and thought leadership content. While it may not be the ideal platform for reaching potential clients directly (unless the office crowd is your cup of tea, which may be no bad thing), it can enhance your clinic's reputation within the industry.

But you can't do everything. Managing multiple social media accounts can be time-consuming, so it's essential to consider your clinic's resources. Determine how much time and effort you can realistically dedicate to social media marketing as this can eat up your evenings at a ridiculous rate, and choose the platforms that best align with your target audience, goals, and resources.

66% of aesthetics practices have a very ad hoc approach to what social content they are going to publish, with no content plan in place.

(MERZ DIGITAL ACADEMY RESEARCH)

It's better to commit to, and excel on, a few platforms rather than stretch yourself too thin across many. Look at the social media channels that other successful aesthetics clinics in your area, or which you admire, are using. What is it that you like about what they do? What is their (no pun intended) overall aesthetic? Don't replicate them completely – you want to establish your own personality online – but there's nothing wrong with a little flattery. The other unique thing about social media is that (unlike, say, your website), performance on social media is very public indeed. You can see exactly what sort of posts are working for competitors because you can tot up the likes and shares. This will give you plenty of insight into the types of content and stories that resonate with your target audience.

Each social media platform offers unique features that can help you market effectively. For example, Instagram Stories and TikTok can be ideal for sharing short, engaging videos showcasing treatments or people-driven stories. Facebook Live, on the other hand, allows you to host Q&A sessions or virtual consultations with potential clients, and "Follow" functions allow you to develop relationships with clients and wider communities for the long term. Investigate the pros and cons carefully.

Once you've chosen the platforms that best align with your target audience, goals, and resources, monitor your performance regularly; but give each channel time to bed down. Online reputations, just like friendships, aren't built overnight, and it will take time, effort and commitment.

Equally, don't be afraid to adapt your strategy if you find that a particular platform isn't yielding results.

AN HONEST LOOK AT INSTAGRAM

Instagram deserves special attention because it's become the go-to platform for aesthetics professionals. It's fast, it's visual, it's elegant, and it's connected to Facebook so it's reasonably well-resourced and easy to use. But that can mean it consumes all your time, effort and budget – and that's not necessarily a good idea. Here are some of the negatives, some of which apply across all social channels, but again, Insta has a hold on many aestheticians' hearts:

- **Don't be fooled:** Experts like me are partly to blame here. Virtually every day, I see adverts promising, "I'll teach you how to build a £million clinic on Instagram alone". It's nonsense – there's no short-cut – it demands hard work.
- **Social is more than Instagram:** If there's one mantra for this book, it's that Instagram is only one of several social media platforms, Social Media is only one of several digital channels, and digital channels are just ONE part of a really strong marketing plan.
- **Insta's reach is in decline:** The ability to reach your existing and potential patients on Instagram is declining annually. As new clinics join, Instagram has to be brutal in deciding whose content should be displayed and in what order. Of course, they prioritise paid posts because they have shareholders to impress. So, it's becoming a highly competitive space.
- **Eggs in one basket:** If you rely on Instagram, an account suspension, deletion, or simply a collapse of the Instagram brand will be disastrous. And trends mean that everything disappears eventually. Remember Myspace? Exactly... Reduce risk by spreading your activity across multiple channels for a balanced approach.

- **Low ROI:** The return on your investment in time and money on Instagram can be relatively low compared to other channels. Remember: views, likes and comments do not equal revenue. Follower numbers and views are just vanity unless they translate into appointments and income. Don't be fooled by your ego!

THE MEGA-LIST OF SOCIAL MARKETING WISDOM

Elsewhere in this book, you'll see that I have tried to create step-by-step processes you can follow to optimise your marketing approaches. Social media is a little different. I feel like there's less of a programmatic approach and that success is more incremental: there are lots of little things you can do, which, when combined, will make a dramatic difference. It's rather like popping pennies into a piggy bank every day and finding that it slowly turns into a sizeable savings pot. In no particular order, then, here is a mega-list of social marketing wisdom.

- **Engagement breeds engagement.** Have you ever noticed how you sometimes see the same people popping up in your social feeds? Do you wonder how they get there? Well, it's you. You have made that happen by engaging significantly with their content. Sometimes "significantly" can mean as little as once. Logic therefore dictates, and experience shows, that the more you interact with your followers, the more of your content they will see in their feeds! So don't just post into the ether and then run – spend some time each day or week engaging with your followers' content. Engage with the followers you want to engage with you in turn: don't waste your time fangirling over another practitioner; go and 'like' a picture of your patient's new kitten!
- **Curate your followers and those you follow.** Be honest with yourself…How many of those you follow are other practitioners? By following them, you're pretty much helping their businesses. What

percentage are customers within a reasonable distance of your clinic? Give both your list of followers and those you follow a healthy purge. Clean out any weird bots while you're at it. It will feel horrible to do this, but it will mean that when you do get engagement, it's real engagement from real people with real reasons to click with you.

- **Be timely.** It's far more effective to post just a couple of times each week, but to do so at exactly the two peak times shown by your stats (most platforms will give you this insight), than it is to post relentlessly at random times which just eat up your time and effort. If you have a big spike in activity on Thursdays at 3 pm, don't question it: that's when you should post! Give yourself the best chance: follow the data.

- **Shortform video is in demand.** Instagram wants Reels (short videos – these also appear on Facebook). Why? Because Insta is in a fight to the death with TikTok, which has become the natural home of short-form videos. Reels get more reach than any other type of post on Instagram, so be sure to use them. This doesn't mean you have to do a full song-and-dance, but Reels are supposed to be entertaining. Consider rapid-cut montages to music, whilst answering educational questions. There are many other options, but be light, branded, entertaining and informative. Make use of captions and hashtags to generate maximum reach, too.

- **Social gets SEO.** Way back in Chapter 2, we looked at Search Engine Optimisation (SEO). It's important to remember that since fairly recently, Instagram and Facebook have both been indexed by Google. This means that what you write on Instagram or Facebook posts (or indeed Reddit and many more) can also appear in search engines. Furthermore, Instagram users can now use the search box to find posts by keywords as well as hashtags. Studies have also shown that people spend longer on posts with long-form copy than ones with just a few lines (that may be a function of the fact that it takes longer to read long posts but proves at the very least that interested people will read!). So, when you're writing the text to go with your images/ animations, etc., don't treat the text as an afterthought; treat it as a crucial indexing opportunity. Include as much detail as possible, and particularly key words and phrases (SkinPen, anti-ageing, etc.). Maximise the depth of valuable detail by following a structure which you can often pre-define. For example, if you are presenting 'Before & Afters' (which are only permitted in some markets, and very rarely permitted in paid-for social media adverts), consider following a structure like this:

- ☐ Explain in detail what the image or case study is about.
- ☐ Provide information on products, treated areas, etc.
- ☐ Explain the treatment experience and time taken, any downtime required, etc.
- ☐ Add a testimonial from the patient if you can.
- ☐ Use hashtags to ensure the content reaches people looking for this information.
- ☐ Use alt tags for images. Alt tags are like hashtags but for pictures – they help your content to show up in Google image searches too.
- ☐ Don't forget to include a call to action – what patients should do if they want to take the next step.

As you can see, there's plenty of basic information you can provide alongside your visuals which will allow for better search engine optimisation and for your posts to be viewed more often.

- ■ **Smash the Hashtags.** Hashtags are live links to link content from all kinds of users around a common theme or topic. They are called hashtags because they begin with a hash, for example, #aesthetics. This uses the hash to denote that the tagged word is important or points to the overall theme of a post. Many services use hashtags to allow users to self-define the themes of a post; for example, "In this post, I'm going to be looking at the #downtime you can expect after a #fillers treatment. #aesthetics" This allows the service (Facebook and Instagram both do this) to index your content more accurately. On Twitter, hashtags are highly searchable. On Instagram, hashtags can even be followed just like an account, and many even have their own "Daily stories". Using hashtags on your post brings you:

- ☐ **Reach:** usually around 25%. Missing hashtags is effectively saying goodbye to a quarter of your potential audience.
- ☐ **Relevance:** Attract new and highly relevant followers from outside of your current audience network as they find your content through their recommended pages or the hashtags they follow, rather than personal connections.

- ■ **Calls to Action.** All good Social Media content has some kind of 'Call To Action'. You are fighting for people's attention amongst the millions of other Instagram posts being injected into their timelines at any given moment, so your duty is to arrest their attention sufficiently to change their behaviour by taking action in a positive way. For example...

- ☐ Tease about new content, treatments, or events before you release the full details. People are curious: teasers work well to create increased engagement around an announcement or new piece of content.
- ☐ Encourage your followers to tag their friends in posts: we all like to help our friends; conversely, nobody wants to look stupid in front of their friends.
- ☐ Use active order prompts, such as "Subscribe to...", or "Register now".
- ☐ Use colour and design techniques – even capital letters – to highlight the call to action in the design of the post.

- ☐ Actually ask for the 'like', 'comment' or 're-post' that you want. Don't ask, don't get!
- ☐ Remind people how easy it is to drop a like (e.g., "double tap this image...")

- **Do a little copywriting.** Similarly, make like a copywriter for maximum engagement. Focus on the user as an individual – use the word "you" when writing copy. Use plain language and avoid jargon (unless you're being helpful and explaining it).
- **Do you (a) like polls, or (b) like polls?** Polls are another great way to build engagement on social media – they are integrated into Twitter and Instagram among others. They are super valuable because you can crowdsource ideas from your audience while being useful to them too. For example, use polls to find out what they want to know and what issues they are concerned about to gauge their reaction to key pieces of information or just to keep people entertained on light-hearted or topical events. Use them to get feedback on your content and generate interaction by "shouting out" and featuring answers and results to polls or standout answers from certain followers (best to get their permission before you share their responses). For a real gold-star response, run polls and then put the correct answer on your website so that users are driven to your website as well as participating. Another social-poll-to-website option is to ask your audience a question in a social poll and then educate them on certain areas of aesthetics by clarifying the correct answer with a follow-up video on your website.
- **Groups (Facebook).** Facebook Groups can be good for your engagement with patients and potential patients. When Facebook started reducing the natural reach of business pages a couple of years ago, they also, at the same time, started increasing the importance of Facebook Groups. This is because a group is a community of like-minded people, something that Facebook want to actively promote.

They changed their algorithm to feature group content much more prominently in users' news feeds and to implement notifications when new content appears in Groups. And that's spot on: Facebook Groups allow you to create a community around your brand in a way that just isn't achievable with a business page or on Instagram. It's a safe and more private place for people to follow what is happening with your clinic and to interact directly with you. Groups now also have Live Video functionality, so it's the perfect architecture to create a sense of exclusivity and privileged access to you and your team. As always, don't use Groups to promote and sell; instead, educate, advise, entertain and engage.

- **Go live!** Speaking of live video, this is the ultimate in engaging formats, even more respected than pre-recorded video content. Whether on Facebook Live or Instagram Live, real-time content provides you with the ultimate in interaction with your patients and followers. Whilst it may not come naturally to you to conduct a live broadcast, nobody needs you to become Dermot O'Leary. It's something you can become comfortable with, and the benefits from an engagement perspective are significant. The algorithms of both Facebook and Instagram favour live content – in fact, they actively encourage it by notifying your followers when you go live. This doesn't happen with regular content and serves to draw people into your live videos very quickly. The ability to see and interact with you through live video means your followers are also more likely to trust you as an authority, which drives up engagement. Use your live shows to run Q&As, give educational content and introduce your opinion on treatment options. See "A sidenote on video", below, for some more help on the practicalities of video production.

- **Saveable Content.** Video not your cup of tea? Instagram is focusing on "carousels" and static images, including infographics. Create saveable images of helpful educational information (based on questions submitted by your followers or leading questions from answerthepublic.com) and create mini guides which can be embedded in 5-to-10-slide carousels.

- **Local Optimisation.** Just as with Google, Instagram has several localising features. Check in to your nearest town when you post, use local hashtags, and use location stickers in your stories. This makes your content more likely to show up in the feeds of people local to you – almost certainly, the highest-value followers you can get. If you haven't read the previous chapter ("Local SEO and local marketing"), you should check it out now!

HOW TO CREATE ENGAGING CONTENT FOR SOCIAL MEDIA

In this section, we'll discuss different types of content that people enjoy, the characteristics that drive engagement, some common pitfalls to avoid, and how to tailor your content to various platforms. Here's what really works in Social Media Land for aestheticians...:

- **Educational content:** Share information about treatments and how they work, healthcare in general and insights that will give customers the comfort to make a purchase. People appreciate content that informs, helps them make better decisions, and enhances their understanding of aesthetics procedures. It'll do your reputation good too.
- **Visual transformations:** Before-and-after images are compelling and will showcase the effectiveness of your services. These visual transformations help potential clients envision the results they can achieve with your team.
- **Personal stories:** Sharing personal stories of clients (with their permission) will create an emotional connection with your audience. Testimonials, case studies, or short interviews can humanize your brand and build trust. Feel free to put your own personal stories up too – what have you been up to recently, which might be of interest?

- **Behind-the-scenes content:** Giving your audience a glimpse of your clinic's inner workings can help them feel more connected to your brand. Share images or videos of your team, treatment rooms, or daily activities to create a sense of familiarity and authenticity.
- **Interactive content:** Social media is meant to be...social! Encourage engagement by asking questions, creating polls, or hosting live Q&A sessions. This interactive content fosters a sense of community, encourages dialogue between your clinic and its audience, and again, will fulfil that all-important educational function.

Making a success of social media is not just about what you say, but also how you say it. Here are some key tips:

- **Authenticity:** Be genuine and transparent in your social media content. Avoid overly promotional posts and focus on sharing high-value information that reflects your clinic's values and personality.
- **Consistency:** Post regularly to maintain visibility and keep your audience engaged. Develop a content calendar to plan your posts and ensure that your content is well-rounded. You can automate social media posts with apps like Buffer so that you don't have to be by a computer 24/7.
- **Quality:** Prioritize high-quality images, videos, and well-written copy. Invest in good equipment, editing tools, or professional help if needed. Aesthetics demands professionalism and attention to detail, and your social activity needs to look just as good!
- **Relevance:** Keep your content relevant to your target audience's interests and needs.
- **Variety:** Mix it up with different types of content and threads of conversation to keep your audience engaged and interested. Experiment with different formats and styles – you'll soon find out what represents you well visually and what works best.

Of course, we also need to offer some advice on what not to do. While it's important to showcase your services, avoid being overly promotional. Unless you're actually advertising, social media is about building relationships – and nobody wants a friend who's trying to sell! Be sure to listen to the responses to your posts, too: social media is a conversation, so don't shout into the ether and then ignore it when people give you an answer. Pay attention to comments, messages, and reviews. Respond promptly and professionally, using feedback as an opportunity to improve your services and content. Finally, beware of plagiarism. Never copy content from other sources without permission or proper attribution. Create original content that reflects your clinic's unique expertise and personality.

We saw above that different platforms have different functionalities. They are also good for different types of content:

- **Facebook:** Share a mix of educational content, personal stories, and visual transformations. Use Facebook Live for Q&A sessions, virtual consultations, or behind-the-scenes content. Engage with your audience by replying to comments and encouraging discussions.
- **Instagram:** Focus on high-quality visuals, including before-and-after images, behind-the-scenes photos, and short videos. Use Instagram Stories and Reels to share more informal, interactive content. Leverage hashtags to increase visibility.
- **Twitter:** Twitter is less about the content than engaging with your audience. Use Twitter polls and threads to encourage interaction and provide more in-depth information. Keep your tweets concise and use hashtags strategically to join relevant discussions.
- **LinkedIn:** Position your clinic as an industry leader by sharing educational content, industry insights, and professional achievements. Engage with other professionals in discussion groups.
- **YouTube:** Create informative longer-form videos on treatments. Offer tutorials, product reviews, or interviews with industry experts

to provide new value to your audience. On YouTube, viewers demand that your videos are well-produced.

■ **TikTok:** Experiment with short, creative video content that showcases your clinic's personality and treatments. Take advantage of popular trends (TikTok is all about virality), challenges, and hashtags to increase visibility and engagement. Keep your content light-hearted and entertaining. This is not the place for your educational content (unless it's dressed up as fun).

A SIDE NOTE ON VIDEO

You'll already know that a mountain of social activity involves video. But you'll be pleased to know that creating great social media videos doesn't always require a large budget or extensive equipment.

In one survey, 64% of businesses said that in the last 12 months, a video on Facebook resulted in a new client.

HTTPS://WWW.HUBSPOT.COM/MARKETING-STATISTICS

You can start with the most basic setup using your smartphone and gradually upgrade to a more advanced setup as your business grows. Here are some options for creating videos, ranging from basic to advanced:

■ **Basic Setup – Smartphone:** A modern smartphone is capable of recording high-quality videos that will be fine for social media platforms. Ensure your phone has a decent camera and consider using a tripod to keep your videos steady. Use the native camera app or explore third-party apps that offer more advanced features and control over your video settings.

- **Intermediate Setup: Smartphone + Accessories:** To elevate your video quality, consider investing in some affordable accessories:

  - ☐ **External microphone:** Improve your audio quality with a clip-on or directional microphone compatible with your smartphone.
  - ☐ **Lighting:** Use natural light whenever possible or purchase a budget-friendly LED light or ring light for more consistent lighting.
  - ☐ **Gimbal:** Keep your videos steady and professional-looking with a smartphone gimbal for smoother movement.

- **Advanced Setup: Dedicated Camera + Accessories:** For an even higher level of video production, invest in a dedicated camera and additional accessories:

  - ☐ **Camera:** Look for a DSLR, mirrorless, or camcorder that fits your budget and offers features like interchangeable lenses, manual settings, and 4K video capabilities.
  - ☐ **Lenses:** Prime lenses typically offer better image quality and better low-light performance.
  - ☐ **Microphone:** Upgrade to a higher-quality shotgun or lavalier microphone for improved audio.
  - ☐ **Lighting:** Invest in a professional lighting kit; softboxes or LED panels will create a warm and visually appealing setup.
  - ☐ **Editing software:** Advanced (and yes, that usually means 'paid for' editing software, such as Adobe Premiere Pro or Final Cut Pro will give you greater control over post-production.

As you progress from a basic to an advanced setup, remember that content and storytelling are still the most critical aspects of any video. Regardless of your equipment, focus on creating engaging, informative, and entertaining videos that resonate. See Chapter 12, Video Marketing, for more on video creation in depth.

MEET YOUR PEOPLE!

The great thing about social media is that it generates content from the one group of people who are even more credible than you: your customers, friends and contacts. Incorporating user-generated content (UGC) and testimonials into your aesthetics clinic's social media marketing strategy can therefore be powerfully persuasive.

User-generated content and testimonials serve as influential tools for promoting your clinic's services, because they provide what marketers call "social proof". Potential clients trust the experiences of others, which helps build credibility and trust in your practice. Furthermore, testimonials offer an authentic perspective on your social group's real-life experiences and their genuine opinions, making them more persuasive than traditional marketing materials.

Sharing user-generated content can also foster a sense of community, encouraging more clients to share their own experiences and increasing overall engagement and brand loyalty. Finally, using UGC and testimonials is also cost-effective, as they can be easily integrated into your existing social media marketing efforts and shouldn't cost you a penny.

To effectively leverage testimonials, invite clients to share their experiences on social media using a branded hashtag or mentioning your clinic's handle or "@name". This will allow you to easily track and collect UGC. You can also offer incentives, such as discounts or exclusive promotions, to clients who share their experiences or submit testimonials. Alternatively, actively request written or video testimonials from satisfied clients through email, social media, or in-person interactions at your clinic. As a matter of courtesy, repay the favour: engage with clients who share their experiences by liking, commenting, and expressing a little gratitude.

Remember to always request permission before sharing a client's content or testimonial on your social media platforms – aesthetics is an intensely personal thing and it's crucial to respect your customers' privacy. With their permission, tag clients featured in your UGC comments to increase visibility and engagement. If naming them is a problem, offer to anonymise them (e.g. using initials: "B. D., Wolverhampton").

Create a dedicated section/page on your website or a social media highlight reel to showcase your testimonials, positive comments or sparks of insight from your clients on sites such as Twitter. Adding context to UGC by including captions or commentary that highlights the specific service or treatment they refer to will create clarity and help potential clients better understand the results they can expect.

Finally, to make the most of your testimonials, incorporate them far and wide; e.g. into your paid social media advertisements, on printed materials, onto your website and more. Beyond before-and-after photos, elements of social proof are consistently the best-performing pieces of marketing you can do.

MAKE SOCIAL WORK IN SYNC WITH YOUR OTHER MARKETING ACTIVITIES

While social media marketing is undoubtedly a powerful tool, it's important not to neglect your other marketing activities. By integrating social media with your other marketing efforts, you can create a cohesive and holistic approach that feels right to your customers and so delivers results.

First and foremost, ensure that your messaging and branding are consistent across all your marketing channels. This includes your website, email marketing, any print materials you produce and social media accounts. Consistency is key to building a strong brand identity (see Chapter 3, above), and it will help you create a lasting impression.

So, when creating content for social media, make sure it reflects the same tone, style, and voice you've used in your other marketing materials. Use the same fonts, graphic style, etc. By doing so, you'll provide a seamless experience for your clients, no matter where they encounter your brand. You'll also be cutting cost and effort out of the process; after all, there's no point reinventing the wheel.

Your socials should also be fully integrated, rather than operating in isolation. Think of your content strategy as a jigsaw puzzle, with each piece representing a different marketing channel. Social media is just one of these pieces, and to create a complete picture, you need to integrate it with your other content efforts. For example, if you publish a blog post on your website, promote it across your social media platforms to drive traffic to your site. Likewise, use social media to gather ideas for new blog topics by monitoring the questions and concerns your clients share online.

Similarly, repurpose content from one channel to another. For instance, turn a popular blog post into a video tutorial for your social media audience. This means you can maximize your content investment and keep your audience engaged across all platforms (meaning, the platforms they most enjoy).

Don't forget to leverage social media as a way to amplify the impact of your traditional marketing too, such as print ads, direct mail, or radio spots. Most practices don't do this sort of thing anymore, but there are plenty of local radio stations in smaller cities that can still represent a good return on ad spend. So, if you do use these channels, whenever you launch a new campaign, create a complementary social media campaign to increase its reach. For instance, if you're running a print ad in a local magazine, share an image of the ad on your social media channels and encourage your followers to share it with their networks. This not only expands the reach of your ad but also adds a layer of social proof to your marketing efforts.

This all applies to email, too. Email marketing remains one of the most effective methods for reaching and nurturing clients. By combining it with social media, you can again create a powerful, interconnected marketing system. Include social media icons in your email newsletters, encouraging your subscribers to follow your clinic on platforms like Instagram,

Facebook, and Twitter. Conversely, use social media to promote your email list by sharing snippets of your newsletter content or offering exclusive incentives for those who sign up.

Finally, as with everything marketing, track the performance of your social integrated efforts. As you can see, there is one overriding message: social by itself will perform to a degree; social plus integration is a real engine for business. By aligning your branding, integrating your content strategy, leveraging social media to support email marketing and amplifying traditional marketing efforts, you'll be well on your way to a holistic – and successful – use of social media.

CHECKLIST

☑ Identify your target audience and determine which social media platforms they like to use.

☑ Create educational, visual, personal, and interactive content that caters to your target audience's interests.

☑ Maintain authenticity, consistency, quality, relevance, and variety in your social media content.

☑ Avoid overly promotional posts and focus on building relationships with your audience.

☑ Tailor your content to the specific strengths and functionalities of each social media platform.

☑ For video content, prioritise storytelling and engagement.

☑ Analyze your competitors' social media strategies and learn from their successes and failures.

☑ Respond to feedback and engage with your audience to foster a sense of community and trust.

☑ Incorporate user-generated content (UGC) and testimonials for social proof.

☑ Invite clients to share their experiences using a branded hashtag or mentioning your clinic.

☑ Repurpose content from one channel to another.

☑ Monitor your social media performance and adapt your strategy as needed to optimize engagement.

INFLUENCER MARKETING

In today's digital age, consumers are increasingly relying on social media platforms to discover new products, services, and experiences. This trend has given rise to a powerful marketing tool that's changing the game for businesses in various industries, including aesthetics practices. Enter influencer marketing.

Influencer marketing involves collaborating with individuals who have established credibility, trust, and influence within a specific community, niche, or industry. These influencers have amassed a significant following on social media platforms, such as Instagram, YouTube, and TikTok, and have the power to impact their audience's purchasing decisions. Partnering with the right influencers can be a highly effective way for aesthetics clinics to reach new clients, strengthen brand awareness, and ultimately, drive growth. Partnering with the wrong influencer can be a waste of time and money.

UNLOCK THE POWER OF TRUST AND AUTHENTICITY

The primary reason why influencer marketing is so effective is that it leverages the trust and authenticity that influencers have built with their followers. In many cases, these followers view influencers as trusted sources of information, opinion, and recommendations. As a result, they are more likely to consider a product or service endorsed by an influencer they admire and respect.

49% of Consumers Depend on Influencer Recommendations.

HTTPS://DIGITALMARKETINGINSTITUTE.COM/BLOG/20-INFLUENCER-MARKETING-STATISTICS-THAT-WILL-SURPRISE-YOU

Influencer marketing is also built on the premise of authenticity. Consumers today are highly discerning and can easily spot inauthentic marketing tactics. Influencers who have built a loyal following have done so by consistently delivering content that their audience trusts. As a result, when an influencer recommends a product or service, it's often perceived as genuine and reliable, rather than a sales pitch.

Influencers come in all shapes and sizes (and, let's be honest, price points). You'll want to identify the best fit for your clinic, budget and the stage of your brand's development. Influencers can be broadly categorized into the following types:

- **Macro-influencers:** These influencers have a large following, typically over 250,000 followers. They often have a broader reach but may have less engagement compared to micro- or nano-influencers. And on the basis of the big numbers, they charge the highest fees.
- **Micro-influencers:** These influencers have a smaller following, usually between 10,000 and 100,000 followers. They tend to have a more targeted audience and higher engagement rates, making them ideal for niche marketing campaigns.
- **Nano-influencers:** These influencers have the smallest following, typically fewer than 10,000 followers. However, they are highly specialized and can have incredibly engaged audiences. Their smaller scale can make them more accessible and cost-effective for partnerships.

Whoever you choose to partner with, there's no one-size-fits-all approach. Depending on your goals and budget, you can choose from several campaign types, which your influencer (or their agent or agency) will execute for you:

- **Sponsored posts:** In this type of campaign, you pay an influencer to create and share a post featuring your product or service on their social media channels. This can include static images, videos, or even live streams.
- **Product reviews:** You can provide an influencer with a sample of your product or service, and in return, they create a review or demonstration video showcasing its benefits and features.
- **Giveaways and contests:** Collaborate with an influencer to host a giveaway or contest, offering your products or services as prizes. This type of campaign can generate buzz and increase your brand visibility.
- **Brand ambassadors:** Building long-term relationships with influencers can lead to them becoming brand ambassadors for your clinic. In this role, they consistently promote your brand to their audience, providing ongoing exposure and credibility.

That brings us to the question of where you're going to promote yourself. Influencer marketing thrives on social media platforms, and each platform offers unique advantages and opportunities. This list is pretty speculative, though, because most influencers will have established their reputations on a particular platform long before you came along, so if you're keen on a particular influencer, they will have made this decision for you. But if you don't mind who the influencer is and want to start with the platform (some influencer agencies work like this), then your options are broadly as follows:

- **Instagram:** With its focus on visual content, Instagram is an ideal platform for showcasing treatment demonstrations. Instagram Stories and Reels are casual and brief.

- **YouTube:** As the world's second-largest search engine, YouTube is a fantastic platform for sharing almost anything – educational content, product demonstrations, etc.
- **TikTok:** Known for its short, engaging video content. Very influencer-friendly and focused on entertaining and inspirational content.
- **Facebook and Twitter:** Although not as focused on visual content, Facebook and Twitter can still play a role in your influencer marketing strategy. They can be used to share blog posts, news, and updates, as well as present the opportunity to engage with your audience through comments and direct messages.

Take a look at Chapter 9, Social Media Marketing, for a deeper dive into the main social channels.

LEGAL AND ETHICAL CONSIDERATIONS

In the UK, influencer marketing is regulated by the Advertising Standards Authority (ASA) and the Competition and Markets Authority (CMA). It's essential for both your clinic and the influencers you work with to adhere to these guidelines to ensure transparency, maintain trust, and avoid potential legal repercussions.

Regulators are keeping a beady eye on influencer marketing because it's had a fairly dubious reputation at times, but the truth is, keeping to the right side of the law is actually better for business than stretching the rules.

Above all, influencers must clearly disclose when they have been paid, gifted, or are otherwise incentivized to promote a product or service. This can be done by using hashtags such as #ad, #sponsored, or #gifted in their social media posts.

Any claims made by influencers about your products or services must also be accurate and it must be possible to substantiate them. Misleading or false claims will lead to legal issues and damage your reputation.

"True influence drives action, not just awareness."

JAY BAER, AUTHOR OF "TALK TRIGGERS"

FIND AN INFLUENCER

Influencers are people – with all the unpredictability that involves. They make mistakes; they get tired; they have egos. Many are young and don't have anyone to look up to because the entire influencer industry has only just sprung up. So don't expect to fall in love with the first influencer you meet, or to enjoy an endlessly professional relationship! Here are some essential factors to consider when identifying the right influencer:

- **Niche:** Choose influencers who focus on your target niche, whether it's anti-ageing treatments, cosmetic procedures or general beauty and wellness.
- **Demographic:** Their audience should align with your clinic's target demographic, otherwise, you're wasting your money!
- **Engagement:** Look for influencers with high engagement rates as this often indicates a strong connection with their followers. High engagement rates translate into better campaign performance and impact.
- **Values and Aesthetic:** Ensure the influencers' values and aesthetic align with your clinic's brand image. This will make the collaboration more authentic and resonate better with the influencer's audience.
- **Authenticity:** Opt for influencers who have a track record of genuine content and honest reviews. This will help maintain credibility with their audience and means a more effective campaign.
- **Location:** When possible, choose influencers based in the same geographic area as your clinic.

- **Gut instinct:** And above all, do you like them? Do you respect and admire them? Do you get a good feeling that they identify well with your brand? And even though they're in it for the money, do you feel that they'll go the extra mile to keep you happy and build a profitable long-term relationship?

If you need help finding influencers, there are lots of online tools to help you. Try Socialbakers, BuzzSumo, or Upfluence for starters.

Also, use a tool like HypeAuditor, to see the true nature and value of an individual influencer's audience. For example, an influencer may have a large following and get plenty of engagement, but if that engagement is coming from middle-aged men while you are targeting women in their 30s, then that influencer isn't going to drive your business forward.

Alternatively, manually search social media platforms using relevant hashtags and keywords. Don't approach the first person you find who looks interesting – this is a competitive business! Do your homework. Research multiple influencers, including their content, values, and audience. Only get in touch with anyone once you've got some benchmarking in place.

When you do make contact, you're fundamentally in a negotiation from the get-go. Personalize your outreach by demonstrating that you have taken the time to understand their work and appreciate what they do. Present a clear value proposition to them by explaining how partnering with your clinic will benefit both them and their audience. This may include offering exclusive discounts, early access to new treatments, or opportunities to use your clinic for content creation, for example. Show that you've thought through where value can lie for both parties. And be transparent: clearly communicate your expectations, campaign objectives you'd like to achieve, and the deliverables you expect them to commit to. Also, discuss what brand commitment you expect: most influencers will rightly demand a significant amount of creative freedom to ensure authenticity in their content.

Finally, think about the long term. Focus on cultivating long-term relationships with influencers, as this will lead to more successful campaigns and ongoing brand advocacy. This matters for two reasons. Firstly, just like advertising, nothing happens overnight. You'll want your influencer to promote you for several months in order for the benefits to bed down. One-hit wonders are extremely rare! So you'll need a strong ongoing relationship. Second, when you both get on, the result will be better than the contract specifies – like a good relationship in any other work context, you'll go above and beyond to help each other, whereas if working together is a chore, nobody will do more than the basics. Stay in touch, support each other and explore opportunities for future collaborations.

DOS AND DON'TS . . .

Be sure to:

- **Set Clear Goals:** Establish clear and measurable goals for your influencer marketing campaign. This will help you evaluate the success of the campaign and provide valuable insights for future collaborations; it will also help your influencer to understand what's expected of them.
- **Define Metrics:** Those goals will likely be based on classic influencer metrics (impressions, engagements, conversions, new client bookings, etc.). There's more on metrics below.
- **Support them:** Offer your tame influencer the necessary resources and support to create high-quality content. This may mean providing product samples, access to your clinic as a video venue, or sharing relevant clinical guidelines. And support them with promotion too – don't forget to retweet and share their work!
- **Be Flexible:** Allow influencers the creative freedom to tailor content to their unique style and audience. That authenticity is part of their product.

And avoid these pitfalls when working with influencers:

- **Don't Micromanage:** While providing guidelines is essential, avoid micromanaging the content creation process. Trust the influencer's expertise and give them the creative freedom to produce content that hits the mark with their audience – because it is indeed their audience first, rather than yours.
- **Don't Neglect Due Diligence:** Perform thorough background checks on potential influencers to ensure their values, ethics and audience align with your clinic's brand. Failing to do so may lead to ineffective campaigns or even damage your reputation: plenty of people claim to be influencers whilst having little true credibility.
- **It's not only about Follower Count:** While it's tempting to choose influencers based on their follower count, prioritise engagement rates and audience fit. Micro- and nano-influencers often have more targeted and engaged audiences, which can lead to better campaign results.
- **Don't Ignore Legal and Ethical Guidelines:** Ensure both your clinic and the influencers you work with adhere to the guidelines set by the ASA and CMA. Proper disclosure and transparency are essential to avoid legal issues further down the line. It's your brand: if you need to educate an influencer on their obligations to keep you on the right side of the law, then make that your business.
- **Don't Rely on Influencer Marketing alone:** While influencer marketing can be highly effective, if there's one thing we've talked about throughout this book, it's that great marketing is multi-faceted. Diversify your marketing to ensure you're reaching your target audience through multiple channels.

THE METRICS OF INFLUENCER MARKETING

Like all marketing, you need to give your influencer activity time to bed down, and then measure your performance (and make changes if you need to!) How do you measure the success of your influencer marketing efforts? In this section, we'll explore the key performance indicators (KPIs) you should track and learn how to make adjustments to improve your campaign's success.

To gauge the effectiveness of your influencer marketing campaigns, it's essential to establish clear KPIs upfront. These metrics will help you assess the performance of your campaigns and inform your future marketing decisions. Here are some KPIs to consider – they are all similar to the advertising, marketing and traffic metrics we've examined earlier.

- **Reach and Impressions:** Reach refers to the number of unique individuals who viewed your (or perhaps more precisely, their) content, while impressions represent the total number of times the content was displayed. By tracking these numbers, you'll understand the extent of your campaign's exposure.
- **Engagement:** This includes likes, comments, shares, and clicks on your content – anything which amounts to involvement and participation from your audience. High engagement rates indicate that the influencer's audience finds your content interesting, and it's meaningful to them.
- **Follower Growth:** A successful influencer marketing campaign should result in an increase in your own social media following. Monitor your follower growth on Twitter, Instagram, TikTok etc. (especially the platform(s) actually used by your influencer, throughout the campaign to determine whether your influencer partnerships are helping you reach a larger audience.
- **Website Traffic:** If your campaign's goal is to drive visitors to your website or e-commerce channels, you'll want to monitor the traffic

generated by your influencer partners. Use tools like Google Analytics to track referral traffic and understand which influencers are driving the most visitors.

- **Leads and Conversions:** Ultimately, you want your campaign to result in new clients for your aesthetics practice. Track the number of leads generated through influencer marketing efforts and the conversion rate of these leads into paying clients.

Understanding your ROI is crucial to determining the success of your influencer marketing campaign, or indeed any other paid activity. To calculate your ROI, you'll need to compare the costs of your campaign to the revenue it generated. Here's a simple formula:

ROI = (Revenue Generated – Campaign Costs) / Campaign Costs

So if you can attribute £1000 of revenue to your influencer and they have charged you £200:

ROI = (£1000 – £200) / £200 = 4 (or 400%)

Remember to account for all costs, including influencer fees, product samples or treatments, and any additional promotional expenses.

A positive ROI indicates that your influencer marketing campaign has generated more revenue than it cost, while a negative ROI means your campaign didn't generate enough revenue to cover the costs. It's essential to analyze your ROI to make informed decisions about your future marketing efforts.

Even with this in mind, the £1000 of revenue this campaign brought in might be deceptive. If the cost of your skincare products, for example, is 50%, then only £500 of this £1000 is actual profit. In that case:

ROI = (£500 – £200) / £200 = 1.5 (or 150%)

After analyzing your KPIs and ROI, make any necessary adjustments to improve the success of your future campaigns. If your metrics reveal that some influencers aren't meeting your expectations, consider ending the partnership or renegotiating terms. Focus on influencers who are delivering results and explore new potential partnerships to expand your reach. Unlike online advertising, this can be painful – real people are involved – but you're running a business not a charity, so make the hard decisions if you have to.

Equally, if engagement with your influencer is high but that's not translating into sales, perhaps it's not your influencer who is at fault but your content, website or products and services. Dig deep to analyse the causes of low (or indeed high) performance.

And as always, test, learn and refine. Influencer marketing is an ever-evolving field, and your strategy should be as well. Continually test different approaches, influencer types, and content formats to discover what works best. Embrace a growth mindset and be open to learning from both successes and failures. There's also nothing wrong with learning from the rest of the market. Keep an eye on your competitors' influencer marketing efforts (after all, it's very public!). Deconstruct their campaigns to identify successful strategies that you might be able to adapt, adopt or improve upon for your own campaigns.

Finally, as we noted above, influencers are people and they respond to loyalty in a way that pay-per-click advertising never will. If you've found influencers who deliver excellent results, consider establishing long-term partnerships with them. This can lead to more authentic content, a better understanding of your brand, and a deeper connection with the influencer's audience. It may also lead to cost savings, as long-term collaborations often result in more favourable terms.

As you continue to explore influencer marketing, keep in mind that more than any other aspect of online marketing, it's a dynamic field that requires ongoing learning, experimentation, and adaptation.

CHECKLIST

☑ Set clear, measurable goals for your influencer marketing campaign.

☑ Research and compare multiple influencers before making contact.

☑ Identify the right type of influencer for your goals, budget, style and target audience. And your gut instinct!

☑ Choose appropriate campaign types (sponsored posts, product reviews, give-aways/contests, brand ambassadors) based on your goals.

☑ Ensure compliance with legal and ethical guidelines.

☑ Allow creative freedom for influencers to maintain authenticity and audience connection.

☑ Focus on cultivating long-term relationships with influencers for ongoing brand advocacy.

MANAGING YOUR ONLINE REPUTATION

In the world of aesthetic practices, where clients trust you with their appearance and self-confidence, your reputation is paramount. Positive online reviews can make all the difference when potential clients are researching and comparing services. In this section, we'll discuss what factors really affect reviews, when and how to ask for a review, and how to collect and use positive reviews.

93% of people read online reviews before making a purchase.

HTTPS://LOCALIQ.COM/BLOG/ONLINE-REVIEW-STATS/

WHAT MAKES CUSTOMERS HAPPY?

Do you do the best job of injecting fillers? Well, guess what? Nobody cares. That is, of course, unfair. It would be more accurate to say nobody knows. Unless there's a genuine disaster, the consumer has no idea whether you're brilliant at the technical side of the job or not.

What they do know is how you make them feel. Here are some of the factors within your control which contribute to a happy customer experience – and none of them are clinical:

- **Attentive, personalised service:** Clients appreciate being treated as individuals, not just another face through the door. Tailor your recommendations and treatments to each client's unique needs and preferences and take the time to make them feel special.
- **Professionalism:** Ensure your staff is well-trained and knowledgeable about your services, treatments, and products. Professionalism also extends to the appearance of your clinic and staff, as well as punctuality and responsiveness.
- **Quality of care:** Consistently deliver excellent results following sound advice and recommendations while minimising side effects. Provide thorough aftercare instructions and support.
- **Transparency:** Be open and honest about treatment costs, potential risks, and expected results. Avoid overselling or making unrealistic promises.
- **Communication:** Actively listen to your clients' concerns and expectations, and communicate in a clear, empathetic manner. Keep clients informed about their treatment progress and answer any questions they may have.

To maximise the number of positive reviews you receive, you're going to want to ask your clients to share their experiences, and that means getting over any (terribly British) discomfort with asking for a recommendation. The best time to ask for a review is soon after the client has completed their treatment and is happy with the results. This is when their satisfaction is at its peak, and they're more likely to provide a glowing review. Whenever possible, ask in person, as this personal touch can be more persuasive. You can do this during the client's follow-up appointment or when they're settling their bill. Make sure to frame the request as a favour that will help your clinic grow and serve more clients.

That said, it's not easy to ask in person and expect a customer to have instant access to their phone or a laptop to finish their review, so you might like to hand out a card with a QR code (those blocky diagrams which turn into links) or a link to your preferred platform for reviews. If asking in person isn't possible or the client needs more time to evaluate their results, send a follow-up email or text message within a week of their appointment. Personalise the message by addressing them by name and reminding them of the specific treatment they received.

Either way, make it easy. Provide clear instructions on how to leave a review and include direct links to your preferred review platforms, such as Google My Business, Trustpilot, or Facebook. This will make the process as straightforward as possible for your clients.

While you should never 'buy' positive reviews, offering a small incentive such as a discount on their next treatment or a free product sample can encourage clients to take the time to share their experiences. Just make sure to mention that the incentive is for leaving a review, regardless of whether it's positive or negative, to maintain ethical standards.

Once you've received positive reviews, make the most of them to boost your clinic's online reputation and attract new clients. Here's what to do with them:

- **Display them on your website:** Showcase your best reviews prominently on your website, either on your homepage or on a dedicated testimonials page. This will help build trust with potential clients who are researching your clinic online.
- **Share them on social media:** Include an image, if possible, to make the post more engaging and visually appealing. Remember to thank the client for their review and tag them if they are happy to do so.
- **Respond to reviews:** Make sure to reply to all reviews, both positive and negative, to show that you value your clients' feedback. For positive reviews, express your gratitude and invite the client to return for future treatments. For negative reviews (see below) respond in a timely and personalised way.
- **Collect video testimonials:** Video testimonials can be particularly persuasive, as they offer a more personal and authentic insight into

your clients' experiences. Not everyone is going to be happy to do this but ask some of your most satisfied clients if they would be willing to provide a short video testimonial and share these on your website and social media channels.

- **Use reviews in marketing materials:** Incorporate positive reviews and client testimonials into your marketing materials, such as brochures, flyers, and email campaigns. This will help reinforce your clinic's reputation more than just about anything else.

- **Analyse the feedback:** Regularly review the feedback you receive from clients to identify areas where you excel and any areas where improvements can be made. This will not only help you maintain a high level of customer satisfaction but also encourage even more positive reviews in the future.

HANDLING NEGATIVE REVIEWS AND FEEDBACK

Despite your best efforts, negative reviews and feedback are inevitable. In this section, we'll discuss effective strategies for handling criticism, keeping customers on your side, and turning these situations into opportunities for growth.

46% of the clinics in a recent survey did not routinely respond to patient reviews online.

(MERZ DIGITAL ACADEMY PROGRAMME RESEARCH)

The first step in handling negative feedback is to avoid taking it personally. Remember that the review is a reflection of the client's experience and not a personal attack on you or your team. Approach the situation with a clear, objective mindset, and focus on finding a solution rather than dwelling on the criticism.

Unfortunately, people are unpredictable; so some negative criticism will also simply be unfair. This small minority of reviews is something you'll just have to suck up.

Promptly addressing negative reviews demonstrates that you care about your clients' satisfaction and are committed to resolving any issues. Keep your responses professional and polite. Avoid using aggressive or defensive language, as this can further escalate the situation and damage your reputation. Begin your response by thanking the reviewer for their feedback and acknowledging their concerns. Show empathy for their dissatisfaction and explain the steps you plan to take to address the issue. If appropriate, invite the reviewer to continue the conversation privately via phone or email.

Take responsibility for any shortcomings and offer solutions. This shows that you're dedicated to continuous improvement and that you value your clients' opinions. Identify the root cause of the problem and outline the measures you'll implement to prevent similar issues in the future.

If possible and appropriate, offer the disgruntled client reasonable compensation for their negative experience, such as a discount on their next treatment, a complimentary service, or a refund. This gesture can help rebuild trust and demonstrate your commitment to customer satisfaction.

The above themes apply to resolving the initial problem and are valuable in their own right. However, to really triumph over adversity, there are further approaches which will help you to run a better business.

Create an environment where clients feel comfortable expressing their concerns directly to your team. This can help prevent negative reviews by addressing issues before they escalate. Train your staff to handle complaints professionally and empower them to resolve issues promptly.

Negative reviews provide valuable insights into areas of your business that need improvement. Use this feedback to assess your services, staff, and overall client experience. Hold team meetings to discuss the feedback and brainstorm ways to enhance your offerings. By turning criticism into an opportunity for growth, you'll be better equipped to prevent similar negative experiences in the future.

And finally, after you've addressed the issues raised in negative reviews, share your improvements with your clients. This can be done through social media updates, email newsletters, or in-person conversations. By highlighting your commitment to customer satisfaction, you can demonstrate that you've taken their feedback seriously and are dedicated to providing the best possible service.

Stay vigilant by regularly monitoring your online reputation. By actively managing your online presence, you'll be better equipped to address concerns promptly and maintain a positive image for your practice. Bad news doesn't have to have a bad outcome; in fact, some of the best customer relationships result from a proactive and positive response to what initially started out as a complaint.

CHECKLIST

☑ Focus on customer experience factors, like attentive service, professionalism, quality of care, transparency, and communication.

☑ The ideal time to ask for reviews is just after clients have completed their treatments.

☑ Make it easy for clients to leave reviews e.g. by providing direct links to review platforms.

☑ Make the most of positive reviews by e.g. displaying them on your website.

☑ Handle negative reviews promptly and courteously, offering a realistic solution.

continued

☑ Create an environment where clients feel comfortable expressing their concerns directly to your team. Train your staff to handle complaints professionally too.

☑ Use negative feedback as an opportunity for growth.

☑ Monitor your online reputation regularly.

Delivering a Black Belt Digital™ workshop to 150 Healthcare professionals in Belfast, 2023

The first Black Belt Digital Event in London (below and opposite)

Black Belt Digital

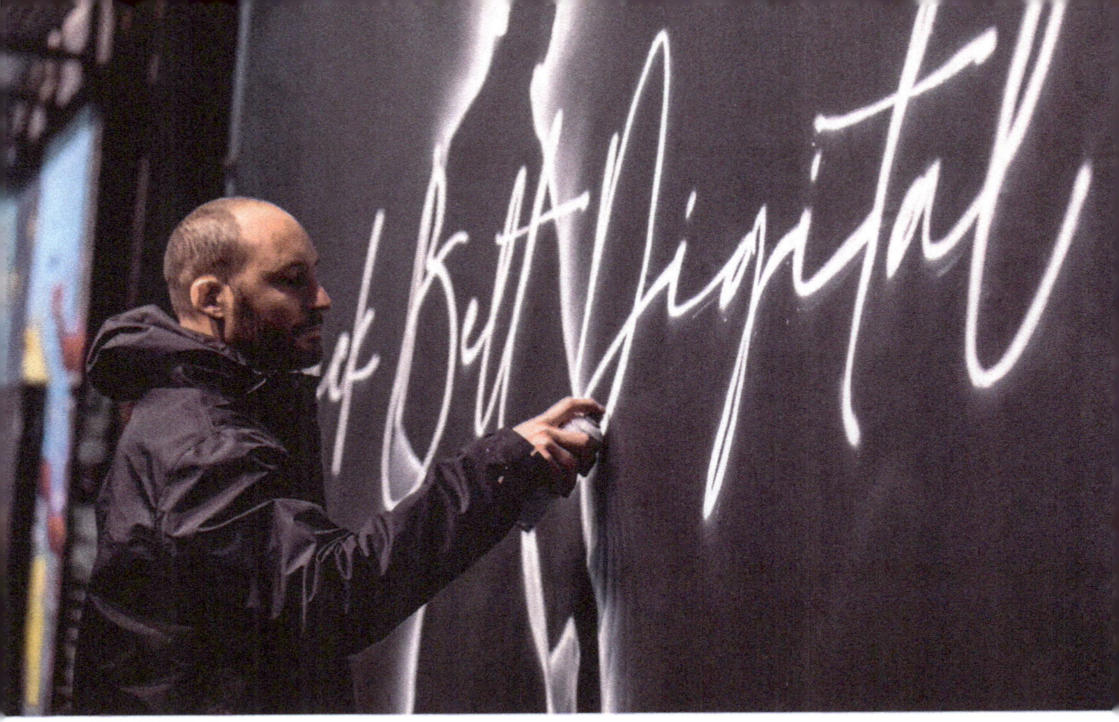
Belt Digital

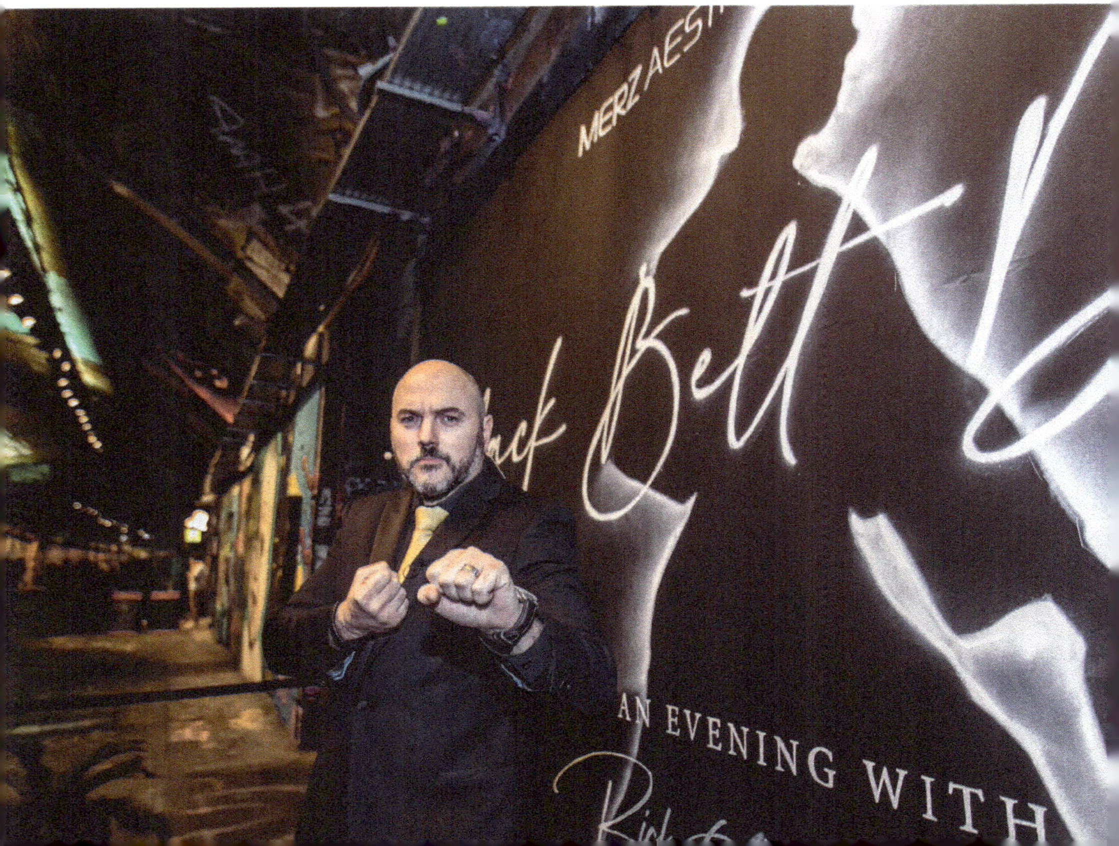
Belt
AN EVENING WITH

Keynote at the Aesthetics Entrepreneurs event

Visiting clients on the bike

Delivering a Digital Marketing workshop to a
room full of Aesthetics Business Owners

Taekwondo Photos

Ricke O'Neill I

PROACTION

With the LTF team and other awesome people from the world of Aesthetics

With the family on a scooter tour of Budapest

My best friend PIXEL,
the Cockapoo

Renewing wedding vows
in Grenada

VIDEO MARKETING

Video marketing has become an increasingly important and effective tool for businesses across various industries (particularly as it's cheaper than ever to get started), and the aesthetics sector is no exception, especially as appearance and transformation are central to the client experience.

The benefits of video marketing for the UK's aesthetics practices are significant. It allows you to demonstrate treatments and procedures, share before-and-after transformations, and highlight the skills of your practitioners, all while engaging potential clients on a deeper, more personal level. A well-crafted video can evoke emotions, tell a story, and ultimately motivate viewers to take action – whether it's booking a consultation, signing up for a newsletter, or following your practice on social media.

88% of video marketers reported that video gives them a positive ROI.

HTTPS://WWW.HUBSPOT.COM/MARKETING-STATISTICS

The rise of social media platforms has made video marketing more accessible than ever. Platforms like Instagram, YouTube, and TikTok have created a vast landscape for marketers to reach and engage with their target audiences. These platforms allow you to share videos that resonate with their interests, preferences and concerns, driving awareness and interest in your practice.

But incorporating video marketing into your overall strategy isn't just about uploading a few clips to social media. To truly harness the power of visual storytelling and stand out in the competitive aesthetics market, it's essential to create engaging, informative, and memorable content that reflects your practice's unique brand identity.

In this chapter, we'll explore some key aspects of video marketing for aesthetics practice managers and cover everything from creating engaging videos and optimizing them for search engines to leveraging social media platforms and keeping up with the latest trends like TikTok. So, let's dive in and start telling your story through the power of video!

MAGIC DUST: CREATING ENGAGING AND INFORMATIVE VIDEOS

There are lots of styles of video to consider – here are some top options:

- **Educational:** These aim to inform and educate your audience; not specifically about your services, but more generally; for example the benefits of treatments and the science behind them. They should be concise, clear, and informative, helping viewers to understand complex topics. Educational videos can include interviews with experts, animations, or demonstrations.
- **Testimonials:** Positive reviews from satisfied clients are a powerful marketing tool (see Chapter 11 – Managing your Online Reputation for more on this). Create video testimonials featuring clients sharing their experiences, the results they've achieved, and their overall satisfaction with your services. Ensure that your clients are comfortable on camera and that their testimonials feel and sound genuine and authentic.
- **Behind-the-Scenes**: Give your audience a glimpse of what happens behind the scenes at your practice. It will give your brand the human

touch. Showcase your team, your workspace, and how hard you work to ensure client satisfaction. This type of video can be more casual and less polished than other formats, which can make it feel more relatable and genuine.

- **Promotional Videos:** These videos are designed specifically to showcase your services, special offers, or events. They should be visually appealing, engaging, and persuasive, enticing viewers to take action. These need to be high-quality and smooth in order to be compelling.

Filming used to be unbelievably expensive. But even though we can now shoot great content on just an iPhone, and therefore, there isn't perhaps such a financial cost to worry about, you don't want to waste time. So before you start filming, it's essential to have a clear plan in place.

Write a script of sorts first. It doesn't have to be every word spoken (in fact, it usually works best if the script contains just bullet points). Your script should outline the content, dialogue, and any visual elements you want to include in your video. Be concise and clear in your messaging, and ensure your script covers all the essential information. Keep your audience in mind and use language that they will understand.

If you're going to get super posh (or visually cool), you might also create a storyboard. This is a visual representation of your script, breaking down each scene into individual shots. This will help you plan the sequence of your video and ensures you have all the necessary shots when filming. You don't need to be an artist to create a storyboard; simple sketches or stick figures will do just fine. A promo video will almost certainly need a storyboard; a simple interview where two heads chat to each other definitely won't. The storyboard is a chance to plan your shots – how are you going to flip between close-ups, medium / two-shots (two people talking), wide shots, action shots etc.... This variety will make your video more visually interesting and help guide the viewer's attention, but it needs to be planned out before you hit the red button.

There's just one more bit of preparation you should do – a rehearsal. Before filming, go through your script and storyboard with your team and any on-camera talent. This will help ensure everyone is on the same page and make the filming process smoother.

If that's the communication creative done, we also ought to look at the technical creative – composition, lighting and sound. There are whole books written about each of these, and we don't have the space here to turn you into Martin Scorsese, but a few starter tips will help you deliver remarkably professional results:

- **Composition** (where people are positioned on the screen): Follow the rule of thirds, which involves dividing your frame into a 3x3 grid and placing your lead subject at the intersections of the grid lines. This creates a more balanced and visually appealing composition. Also, ensure there is enough headroom to avoid awkward framing.
- **Lighting:** Use natural light when possible, but also consider investing in affordable lighting equipment, such as softboxes or LED panels. Ensure your subject is well-lit and avoid harsh shadows or over-exposure. Weak composition won't ruin your film; weak lighting will.
- **Sound:** Clear audio is also essential for a successful video. In fact, viewers notice (and switch off) bad sound even more than bad lighting. Invest in a good-quality external microphone (lavalier or shotgun) to capture crisp audio. Avoid filming in noisy environments and be aware of any background noises that could be distracting or make it difficult to hear the speaker.
- **B-roll footage:** B-roll is supplemental footage that supports your primary video content. It can be used to show different angles, illustrate points, or add visual interest. It can be as simple as a wide shot of a location or your subject walking or nodding in agreement. Capture B-roll footage during your shoot and use it to enhance your final video during the editing process.

- **Editing:** Once you've captured all of your footage, it's time to edit your video. There are several affordable and user-friendly video editing software options available, such as Adobe Premiere Pro, Final Cut Pro, and DaVinci Resolve. Editing is an art in itself, but broadly edit your video to ensure a smooth flow, remove any errors or awkward pauses, balance being interesting and varied against the expense of filming, and add graphics, text, or animations as needed if you can.

That's an unbelievably whistlestop tour of filming, but in short, creating engaging and informative videos for your aesthetics practice requires a bit of planning, effective storytelling, and attention to detail. What it doesn't require is tons of new equipment. Experiment, have fun, and see what works for you.

DIY VIDEO PRODUCTION TECH AND TOOLS FOR THE BUDGET-CONSCIOUS MARKETER

Creating high-quality videos for your aesthetics practice doesn't have to break the bank. With the right tools and techniques, you can produce engaging and professional videos on a budget. In this chapter, we'll explore DIY video production technologies, tips for creating marketing videos at scale, and when and how to seek expert help. Let's go shopping for:

- **Camera:** While many smartphones today offer excellent video quality, investing in a DSLR or mirrorless camera with interchangeable lenses will provide more control and better results. Consider purchasing a camera with 4K video: the file sizes are huge, but its greater resolution allows for more flexibility in post-production.
- **Audio equipment:** As mentioned in the previous section, clear audio is crucial for successful videos. Invest in an external microphone to capture high-quality sound. Additionally, consider purchasing a

portable audio recorder to capture separate audio tracks, allowing for more control during editing.

- **Lighting:** Affordable lighting options or even ring lights which improve your appearance on a smartphone, can make a big difference in your video quality. Experiment with different lighting setups to find the most flattering and visually appealing look for your videos. Note that lighting is particularly important in aesthetics, as skin tones are literally what your audience is most interested in!

- **Tripod or stabilizer:** Stabilizing your camera is essential for professional-looking videos. Invest in a sturdy tripod or, if you plan on shooting handheld, a gimbal or other stabilizing equipment.

- **Editing software:** Video editing software is essential for assembling and polishing your footage. Above, we mentioned Adobe Premiere Pro, Final Cut Pro, and DaVinci Resolve; more budget-friendly alternatives include iMovie and Shotcut.

- **Stock footage and music:** To add variety and interest to your videos, consider using stock footage and music. Many websites offer royalty-free assets at affordable prices or even for free. Just make sure to check the licensing terms to ensure you're using the content legally. For example, many stock libraries allow you to use their creativity for educational purposes, but not for advertising.

As well as cutting costs (not corners!) on equipment, you can also cut costs on your ways of working to scale up your production process, reducing your cost-per-video.

To save time and resources, consider filming multiple videos in one session. Set aside a day or two for video production and plan your shoots so that you can efficiently capture footage for several videos at once. This batch production will also help maintain consistency in your style and quality across your videos.

You should absolutely also reuse and repurpose the content you shoot. Maximize the value of your video content by repurposing it for different platforms and formats. For example, you could create shorter versions of your videos for social media, turn an interview into a podcast episode, or add B-roll footage to existing materials to produce a promotional film.

Cut the time you take on editing, etc., with templates and presets for elements like titles, graphics, and colour grading. This will save you time but comes with the additional benefit of ensuring a consistent look across your videos. Presets defined by the software are also usually pretty tried-and-tested, giving you a benchmark look and feel to work from.

Finally, involve your team members in the video production process, from brainstorming ideas to assisting with filming or editing. This can help distribute the workload and bring new perspectives to your content; and to be honest, filming is fun. It's a positive experience which really brings a team together.

All that said, while DIY video production is an excellent option, there are times when hiring a professional is a smart idea. Go with home production for as long as you can (unless you've got a friendly local professional prepared to help you out!) but get help when you hit these challenges:

- **Complexity:** If your project requires advanced skills, specialized equipment, or a large-scale production, hire a professional video production company.
- **Time constraints:** If you're short on time or need to produce a high volume of videos quickly, outsourcing the work to experts can help ensure you meet your deadlines without compromising on quality.
- **Brand image:** Low-quality videos will impact your brand image. If you're launching a major campaign or targeting a high-end clientele, investing in professional video production may be a wise decision.

If you can, go with a friend or a recommendation from a friend. If you can't, research top-quality freelancers. Look at their portfolios, client testimonials, and case studies to assess their quality of work and make sure their style aligns with your brand. Remember, you can pay for the very best, but if their style and vibe are different to yours, you'll just be disappointed. It's fine to request proposals: reach out to several potential partners and ask for an outline of their approach, timelines, and cost estimates for your project. Be as specific about your objectives and requirements as you can. Evaluate each proposal based on factors like cost, experience, creativity, and alignment with your brand. Consider the value they can bring to your project, not just the price tag. Even so, don't underestimate the value of a conversation. Meet your top choices and go with your gut instinct after making sure you're comfortable with any terms, payment schedules and intellectual property or licensing considerations.

So what have we learned? When the time is right, you can get help. But above all, producing engaging and high-quality videos for your aesthetics practice is achievable even on a budget. With the right DIY tools and techniques, you can create content that will effectively attract new clients.

OPTIMIZING AND PROMOTING YOUR VIDEOS

Shooting and editing so you get to a gorgeous creative is only the start. To maximize the impact of your video marketing efforts, it's essential to optimize and promote your content effectively.

For starters, subtitling is crucial for making your video content accessible to a broader audience. That's not just the deaf or hard of hearing or non-native speakers in our global world of content. Now that we're watching video on smartphones, we're watching it in more places. 69% of people view video with the sound off in public places and 25% also watch with the sound off in private. Subtitles are, therefore, pretty important.

To create accurate and well-timed subtitles, consider using subtitling tools like: Rev.com (professional subtitling with quick turnaround times), Kapwing (the DIY option – a user-friendly online editor for creating and editing subtitles) or Amara (a collaborative subtitling platform that allows users to create and edit subtitles together).

For accessibility purposes, you should also invest in some further elements of video augmentation. In addition to captions, be mindful of colour contrast when creating visuals for your videos. This is especially important for text, as poor contrast can make it difficult for viewers with visual impairments to read. Also, consider offering transcripts of your videos. Transcripts make your content accessible to people who prefer to read or use screen readers due to visual impairments or difficulties due to dyslexia; they're also searchable, which means they're useful for SEO.

This brings us to SEO in general. Video is like every other form of content, in that search engine optimization (SEO) is crucial for increasing the visibility of your videos in search results, ultimately driving more views and engagement. We cover the general rules of SEO in Chapter 3, Your Website, however, there are some extra steps to optimizing your video content with SEO and keywords:

- **Optimize video titles:** Create compelling and descriptive video titles that include your target keywords. This will make your videos more appealing to potential viewers and help them to rank higher in search results.
- **Write detailed descriptions:** Craft informative video descriptions that provide context and incorporate your target keywords (just like the meta text you should be using on your web pages). This not only helps search engines understand your video content better but also gives viewers an idea of what to expect, increasing the likelihood they'll watch.
- **Use tags strategically:** On platforms like YouTube, use relevant tags to further optimize your video for search. Include your target keywords and related terms to help your video appear in the right search results and "Suggested video" lists. (By the way, don't be tempted to scam these descriptions and tags with something like "Free champagne on a speedboat", unless you really are offering free champagne on a speedboat. Disappointed viewers will switch off, the platform

will notice this fact, and they will actually deprioritise your videos. Honesty is definitely the best policy!)

- **Add captions and transcripts:** As noted above, including captions and transcripts not only improves accessibility but also helps search engines better understand your video content, positively impacting your SEO efforts.

- **Create engaging thumbnails:** Design eye-catching custom video thumbnails that accurately represent your content and include your target keywords in the file name. This can help improve click-through rates and drive more views.

- **Optimize video length:** While there's no one-size-fits-all answer for video length, consider your audience's preferences and the platform you're using. Longer videos may rank better on YouTube, while shorter, more engaging content may perform better on social media platforms like Instagram and TikTok.

In fact, you're probably going to use more than one social media platform for video. Here are the major options:

- **YouTube:** As the world's largest video-sharing platform, YouTube should be a cornerstone of your video marketing strategy. Create a professional and well-organized YouTube channel, complete with a profile picture, banner, and channel description. Optimize your video titles, descriptions, and tags as mentioned earlier. Encourage viewers to like, share, and subscribe to your channel, and engage with them in the comments section to foster a sense of community. Note that YouTube videos are incredibly easy to share too – both for you to embed in your website and for customers to share with their friends and families.

- **Instagram:** Instagram offers multiple ways to share video content, including feed posts, Stories, IGTV, and Reels. Each format has its advantages and is suited to different types of content. Feed posts are ideal for showcasing high-quality, evergreen content, while Stories allow for more informal, behind-the-scenes glimpses into your practice. IGTV is great for longer, educational videos, and Reels are perfect for short, fun clips.

■ **TikTok:** This short-form video platform has grown like…well, it depends on your perspective. We'll cover TikTok more below.

■ **Facebook:** Share your video content on your practice's Facebook page and consider using Facebook Live for real-time engagement with your audience. Facebook's video platform also supports captions, making it easy to improve accessibility.

■ **Twitter:** Share your videos on Twitter, using relevant hashtags to increase visibility. Twitter also supports captions, enabling you to make your videos more accessible.

Don't limit your videos to just one platform. Cross-promote your content across multiple channels to maximize reach and engagement. Be sure to tailor your videos and captions to each platform's unique requirements and audience preferences.

Wherever you put your videos, you'll want to see how well they do. As with every marketing segment we've looked at in this book, there's always a suite of metrics there to help you with the numbers. The actual tools will vary platform by platform, but here are some key metrics to track and analyze:

■ **Views:** Track the number of views your videos receive to gauge their overall reach and visibility.

■ **Watch time (aka 'Dwell time'):** Analyze the average watch time of your videos to determine how well your content is holding your viewers' attention. If you notice a significant drop-off at specific points, consider adjusting your content or presentation style.

■ **Engagement:** Monitor likes, comments, and shares to measure audience engagement with your videos. High engagement rates indicate that your content is resonating well.

- **Click-through rate (CTR):** Track the CTR of each video's call-to-action (CTA) to measure the effectiveness of your messaging and the likelihood of viewers taking the desired action.
- **Conversion rate:** Monitor the number of leads or sales generated by your video marketing efforts to assess their impact on your bottom line.
- **Audience demographics:** Take an occasional look at the demographics of your viewers to make sure you're reaching your target audience and not wasting money on beautiful content which brings in the wrong people.
- **Traffic sources:** You may also be able to see where your video views are coming from – whether it's organic search, social media platforms, or other sources, e.g., links. This will help you identify which platforms and strategies are driving the most traffic and engagement.

In the rest of this chapter, we'll explore two additional ways to utilize video marketing for your aesthetics practice: (1) video advertising and (2) live streaming and webinars. These methods can help you reach new audiences, drive conversions, and deepen your connection with existing clients. But first, let's meet the new kid on the block.

FIND OUT WHAT MAKES TIKTOK TICK

TikTok has taken the world by storm, captivating users with its short-form videos and personalized stream. So, I think it deserves a special mention. With a rapidly growing user base, it can't be ignored and represents a unique opportunity for aesthetics practices to connect with new audiences.

Begin by creating a professional account for your aesthetics practice, complete with a username based on the business, profile picture, and a compelling bio that highlights your services and expertise. Link to your website or other social media profiles to ensure potential clients can easily find more information when they want it. In this sense, TikTok is no different to other social media sites.

———————

**72% of respondents found ads on TikTok 'inspiring',
the highest across all platforms.**

HTTPS://WWW.SOCIALMEDIATODAY.COM/NEWS/TIKTOK-SHARES-NEW-AD-STRATEGY-
TIPS-BASED-ON-RESPONSES-FROM-25000-USERS/598338/

———————

**"TikTok users are in a discovery mindset when scrolling through
the For You feed, and receptive to new and inspirational videos
from creators and brands alike."**

KANTAR RESEARCH

———————

But one of the keys to TikTok's success is understanding and embracing the platform's unique culture. Unlike other social media, TikTok thrives on trends, challenges, and popular sounds/memes. By participating in these trends, you'll increase the visibility of your content and make it more discoverable to users, thanks to TikTok's other big draw: a truly addictive algorithm.

Make sure that your participation aligns with your practice's image and values; but if you can hang onto the coattails of an emerging trend, the benefit can be extraordinary. Use relevant and popular hashtags in your video captions to increase visibility and reach based on these trends.

As you develop your TikTok content, focus on showcasing your practice's services, offering helpful tips, and highlighting your team's expertise. While you can certainly take inspiration from popular content ideas, such as before-and-after transformations or Q&A sessions, remember that authenticity is key on TikTok, and staying true to your brand will help you build a loyal following.

TikTok culture is also known for its highly interactive nature, so make sure to engage with your viewers by responding to comments, answering questions, and acknowledging their feedback. Building a sense of community around your aesthetics practice will help foster loyalty and encourage user-generated content featuring your services.

Collaborating with TikTok influencers in the beauty and aesthetics space can also help expand your reach and introduce your practice to new audiences. Carefully research potential partners based on their audience demographics, engagement rates, and content quality to ensure a successful partnership. That said, note that the numbers for TikTok are huge at the moment – influencers can be ridiculously expensive, but aesthetics is a very attractive sector for this sort of engagement.

As always, sharing is good. To amplify your TikTok presence, share your videos across your other social media profiles, website, and email marketing. This cross-promotion will drive traffic to your TikTok profile and help you establish a strong presence on the platform (and that applies equally to other platforms too). If you're looking to reach an even larger audience, consider investing in TikTok ads. The platform's ad formats include In-Feed Ads, Branded Hashtag Challenges, and Branded Effects, all of which have different fees and offer different outcomes.

Like all platforms, TikTok demands effort to understand and leverage. Above all, embrace its unique culture, short-form delivery and focus on authentic, engaging content.

SIDE NOTE: VIDEO ADVERTISING

If you want to create video ads, there are definitely some extra rules to consider. Follow these tips to create compelling video ads that drive conversions:

- **Keep it short and focused:** Most video ads should be between 10-30 seconds, depending on the platform and ad format. Keep your ad concise and focused, clearly conveying your message and value proposition within this limited timeframe.

- **Hook viewers in early:** Capture your audience's attention within the first few seconds of your ad. On YouTube, for example, many ads can be skipped after 5 seconds. Use strong visuals, compelling questions, or intriguing statements to encourage viewers to keep watching, or they'll be gone.

- **Showcase your best bits:** Clearly communicate what sets your aesthetics practice apart from the competition. Highlight your expertise, technology or customer satisfaction to create a compelling argument for choosing your services.

- **Include a strong call-to-action:** Encourage viewers to take the next step by including a clear call-to-action (CTA) in your video ad. This could be a prompt to visit your website, schedule a consultation, or sign up for a special offer. It'll only be a click, but you need to think about what will encourage that click.

- **Optimize for silent viewing:** We mentioned this earlier – it's even more important for advertising. Many viewers watch videos with the sound off, especially on social media platforms. Ensure your ad's visuals and captions effectively convey your message, even without audio.

SIDE NOTE: LIVE STREAMING

Live streaming and webinars offer unique opportunities to engage with your audience in real-time, adding value to their experience and building your brand. Here are some tips for successful live events:

- **Get the basics right.** Like any piece of content, choose a relevant topic that's valuable to your target audience, for example, a demonstration of a new treatment, an educational presentation or a Q&A session with an expert. Promote your webinar properly across your website, email list, and social media channels. Provide clear information about the date, time, and how to join, and consider offering an incentive for attendees, such as a discount or giveaway. Make sure you're well-prepared – rehearse any presentation to ensure a smooth delivery and do a run-through to anticipate any potential technical issues.

- **Get the right kit.** Streaming doesn't need dramatically more equipment than shooting a standard video (we covered a basic kit list earlier in this chapter), but it does deserve special consideration. If you can go with a camera with good low-light performance (or a low-light setting) and autofocus capabilities, that's particularly desirable. As we've already said on audio, avoid relying on built-in microphones as they usually produce subpar sound quality. You will need to test that you've got good connectivity, though. That means a reliable computer or laptop with sufficient processing power and RAM to handle video streaming without lag or stuttering; and a stable, high-speed internet connection (preferably wired) to ensure smooth streaming and minimal buffering. Finally, you'll need a webinar platform or streaming software (e.g. Zoom, Webex or OBS Studio), to host, manage, and broadcast your webinar.

- **Engage your audience:** Encourage interaction during your live event by asking (or taking) questions, soliciting feedback, and responding to comments. This will create a more engaging experience and foster a sense of community among attendees.

- **Offer a replay:** After your live event, make the recording available for those who were unable to attend. This allows you to reach a larger audience and provides additional content for your marketing efforts.

- **Follow up:** After the event, follow up with attendees by sending a thank-you email, providing additional resources, and encouraging them to take the next step, such as scheduling a consultation or signing up for your newsletter.

CHECKLIST

☑ Plan carefully! Write scripts, storyboard if necessary, and rehearse with your team.

☑ Invest in affordable DIY video production tools – you don't have to be Tarantino from day one.

☑ Implement time and money-saving strategies: Batch production, repurposing content, using templates/presets, etc.

☑ Know when to get professional help (e.g. complex projects, high-end campaigns).

☑ Optimize for SEO: Create compelling video titles, detailed descriptions, strategic tags, engaging thumbnails, and consider video length to improve search engine visibility.

☑ Share your videos on Instagram, YouTube, TikTok, and other platforms.

☑ Add subtitles!

☑ Track key metrics: views, watch time, engagement, click-through rate, conversion rate.

☑ Embrace TikTok's unique trend-based culture, especially for a younger audience.

☑ Engage with your audience: respond to comments and acknowledge feedback.

☑ Collaborate with influencers in the beauty and aesthetics space to expand your reach.

TRAINING AND EDUCATIONAL MARKETING

One often overlooked but highly effective strategy is educational marketing. It establishes credibility and authority – by providing your potential and existing clients with valuable educational content, you position yourself as an expert in the aesthetics field. This creates trust and fosters a sense of authority, encouraging clients to choose your practice over competitors who may not be sharing the same level of knowledge. That's particularly true in aesthetics, where trust counts for a lot in customers' eyes.

Educational materials also help clients to make informed decisions about their aesthetic treatments, so it also serves to push customers towards a sale. By offering them resources to understand the procedures, benefits, and any potential risks, you empower them to feel more confident about their choices, leading to greater satisfaction with your services. These are also the people who will recommend your practice to friends and family. This increases your client base and enhances your industry reputation. Basically, being an expert and being perceived as an expert, is good for your image and your business.

Consumers are 131% more likely to buy from a brand immediately after they consume early-stage, educational content.

HTTPS://WWW.CONDUCTOR.COM/ACADEMY/
WINNING-CUSTOMERS-EDUCATIONAL-CONTENT/

All that said, we're going to go into a fair amount of detail here, and not all of it will be relevant unless you have fairly deep pockets and want to put education at the heart of your brand.

If you just scribble a few educational blogs, that will do just fine for many practices (and the content advice I present here will be very useful). If you want to go further, there's more material here about how to structure educational materials and how to use them to engage most effectively.

DEVELOPING EDUCATIONAL CONTENT

The rules for developing educational content are largely the same as those for developing marketing content in general, but with some extra emphasis – because nobody wants to feel like they're thick! Learning, even if it's just reading a guide, shouldn't feel like too much effort, and also shouldn't feel so easy that it's patronising. The result is a bunch of ideas called "Instructional design" – officially defined as "the creation of learning experiences and materials resulting in the acquisition and application of knowledge and skills". This is pretty impenetrable in itself – so let's keep it simple, with the basics of instructional design for salespeople rather than educators:

- **Choose topics that resonate** with your audience: Producing educational materials comes at a cost – especially if you use multimedia – so choose topics that are laser-focused in relevance to your audience's interests and concerns. This may include information on specific treatments, tips for maintaining results, or news and trends in the aesthetics industry.
- **Use a mix of content formats:** To cater to different learning styles and preferences, use a variety of content formats, e.g. blog posts, videos, infographics, and social media posts. This ensures that your educational marketing efforts are engaging and accessible to a wide range of clients.

- **Keep it simple:** Avoid using jargon or overly technical language. Use simple, concise language to explain concepts and procedures. This keeps your content accessible and easy to understand.

- **Use real-world examples:** This is so important and so easy to achieve. Incorporate relatable examples and case studies to help illustrate key concepts and ideas. This can help clients better understand the benefits of specific treatments and procedures, as well as the potential risks and outcomes. By sharing relatable success stories and testimonials, you can create a more compelling narrative that resonates.

- **Organize content logically:** Structure your educational materials in a way that is easy to follow and understand. Break down complex concepts into smaller, manageable sections, and use headings and subheadings to guide the reader through the content. This will make it easier for your audience to digest and retain the information.

- Similarly, use every trick in the book to **make content easy to navigate**. Use headings and subheadings so users can skim through the content to find specific topics or sections that interest them or solve their problems. Include a table of contents or navigation menu. And use plenty of lists and bullet points – they are an excellent way to present information in a concise and easy-to-read format.

- **Incorporate visuals:** Visual aids, like images, graphics and diagrams, can help clarify complex concepts and make your content more engaging. Use visuals strategically to support and enhance text, while ensuring that they are always relevant and of high quality.

Now, I don't want to get all cocky here, but if you look at this book, it follows many of the principles listed above – because it's an educational book. Everything here is bite-sized, organised and signposted. It's simply written, avoids jargon and is designed to be practical, not academic.

If you plan to create a few educational blogs, articles or e-books, then the above advice will serve you well. If you intend to delve a little further by creating specifically educational experiences which are evolved beyond just the provision of content, then the following can be added to the list:

- **Promote interaction and engagement:** Encourage your audience to engage with your content by including interactive elements such as quizzes, polls, or discussion forums. This makes the learning experience more enjoyable and helps reinforce key concepts and so improves retention.
- **Provide opportunities for practice and reinforcement:** Offer practical exercises, simulations, or case study work-throughs that allow your audience to apply what they have learned in a safe and controlled environment. This helps to reinforce learning.
- **Offer feedback and support:** If you're really devoting time to education, provide your audience with opportunities to ask questions and get clarification on your materials. Use Q&A sessions, webinars, or even one-on-one consultations. This will, of course, eat up time, so this is only for you if you're putting an advisory function at the heart of your marketing.

You'll also need to shake things up a bit with multiple types of content. Classic articles and blogs are absolutely fine, but also consider:

- **E-books:** A popular choice for written content, as they can be easily accessed on most devices and are convenient for users to consume information at their own pace. E-books are particularly suitable for in-depth guides, how-to manuals, and other comprehensive resources.
- **Webinars:** Live, interactive online events that allow you to present information and engage with your audience in real-time. It's an excellent format for demonstrating techniques, hosting Q&A sessions or interviewing other experts. Webinars can be recorded and shared for those who are unable to attend the live event.

■ **Video courses:** Video courses are ideal for explaining complex concepts or demonstrating practical skills. Video courses can be pre-recorded and broken down into smaller modules, allowing users to progress through the material at their own pace. We'll come back to video, podcasts and interactive tools in a little more detail below.

STORYTELLING

A compelling story is a powerful tool in marketing. We've already seen elsewhere here that your story is an important part of your brand, and in general, the story behind a product is more valuable than its ingredients or what it will do for the buyer!

"Marketing is no longer about the stuff that you make, but about the stories you tell."

MARKETING GURU, SETH GODIN

Storytelling engages your audience and makes your content more memorable. By incorporating storytelling into your content, you can make complex concepts more relatable and enjoyable. So, develop a narrative: present your information in a way that tells a story, with a clear beginning, middle, and end. This makes it much easier to show why a story was worth telling. It also means users will connect with the information you give them on an emotional level, and that makes your content much more engaging, relatable and memorable.

We talked above about using case studies and real-life examples – sharing stories from your own experience is obviously a good way to start. But feel free to go further, especially if you're on video (which gives you a lot more flexibility on tone and how you communicate). Use metaphors and analogies and draw comparisons like "On the one hand, X, on the other hand, Y", to lead readers/viewers through complex concepts. Storytelling is the heart of the educational sell.

USING MULTIMEDIA

Different people have different learning styles, and incorporating a variety of multimedia elements into your content will help cater to these preferences. By using text, images, videos, and audio, you can create a richer learning experience and keep your users engaged. But you equally don't want to be spending all your budget on innumerable different ways of saying the same thing. Use the lists below to settle on what you can comfortably and cost-effectively deliver:

- **Use videos for demonstrations:** If your content includes practical tips or techniques, consider creating video demonstrations to show users exactly what to do or what it will feel like. Videos can be especially helpful in the aesthetics industry, as they allow users to see the results of treatments and procedures and to understand what they will experience (which minimises fear and worry).
- **Incorporate audio content:** Audio content, such as podcasts or narrated presentations, are more engaging for "auditory learners" but more importantly, it's an excellent way for users to consume information while multitasking or on the go. Podcasts are currently thriving, and they're increasingly cheap to produce, so if you haven't given audio a thought recently, it might be worth your while.
- **Interactivity is about fun:** Interactive elements, such as quizzes, polls, or simulations, are not just there to educate or test knowledge. They're bitesize lumps of fun, making learning more enjoyable.
- **Combine multimedia formats:** Use a mix of text, images, videos, and audio to create a comprehensive and engaging learning experience.
- **Keep multimedia elements relevant:** Ensure that any multimedia elements you include are relevant to the topic you're discussing and

contribute to the user's understanding of the material. For example, if a complex concept with lots of interactions needs demonstrating onscreen, a podcast won't be your best choice. In the same way, avoid using multimedia simply for the sake of visual interest; it should always serve a purpose in enhancing the learning experience.

- ■ **Accessibility:** Finally, make sure your multimedia content is accessible to users with disabilities. Provide alt text for images, closed captions for videos, and transcripts for audio content. This ensures that your content is inclusive and can be enjoyed by a wider audience.

Before going crazy on a multimedia blitz, remember – you're still only marketing. Every penny you spend counts. Consider the age, interests, and technological capabilities of your target audience – what types of content are they most likely to engage with and find useful? What do you want them to walk away understanding? – because here there will be two answers, a learning outcome and a marketing outcome.

Determine what you can realistically create and maintain within your budget and time constraints, and also remember that you should ultimately be looking to create more than one content asset – it's unlikely that a single video or blog is going to establish your reputation as a trusted authority.

Finally, remember that some platforms (by which I mean both website platforms like WordPress and learning platforms like eduMe and Tovuti) have limitations on the types of multimedia content they can support. Check the capabilities of the platform you plan to use before investing in multimedia elements.

PLATFORMS

Most marketers don't need to invest in education delivery platforms (also known as LMS – Learning Management Systems), but it's worth a look at them and how they overlap with classic social media. We are, after all, just creating content which we want to distribute widely.

So the first point to make is that you likely don't need a platform at all. Depending on your goals and resources, you may opt to host your educational content directly on your website or blog. This is cost-effective and allows you to maintain control over your content, although it also means that promoting it is your problem too.

Micro-content platforms like social media (Instagram, Twitter, and LinkedIn) are perfect for sharing bite-sized pieces of educational content – or perhaps I should say, bite-sized pieces of educational content are ideal for sharing on social media. We've looked at these platforms above in Chapter 9 (Social Media). They are ideal for helping you to build brand awareness and engagement, and for simple pieces of content. They're less suitable for hosting more extensive or in-depth materials.

Larger pro platforms, like YouTube, Udemy, or Teachable, offer a more comprehensive solution for hosting and distributing educational content. These platforms often provide built-in tools for organising and marketing your content, as well as access to a broader audience. However, they may also involve fees or revenue-sharing arrangements, and you may have less control over your content's presentation and user experience.

When evaluating platforms, here are a few points to consider:

- **Audience reach:** How easily can your target audience access and discover your content, and how many people can you reach? (Here, YouTube is probably the undisputed champion.)
- **Functionality and ease of use:** Does the platform provide the necessary tools and features to create, organise, and deliver your content effectively? After all, do you really want to be knee-deep in learning a whole new platform?
- **Cost:** What are the costs associated with using the platform, do they align with your budget and objectives, and can they beat the free option of doing nothing or popping educational materials into a blog?

- **Control and customisation:** How much control do you have over the presentation of your content and the user experience? Can you customise the platform to align with your brand and aesthetics practice's image?
- **Integration:** Can the platform be easily integrated with your existing website, marketing efforts, and analytics tools?
- **Support and resources:** Does the platform offer sufficient support and resources to help you succeed in your educational marketing efforts?

Finally, using a combination of platforms, media and your website is likely to be the most effective approach. For example, you could create an e-book containing in-depth information on a specific treatment, then promote it on your website and social media channels. You might then host a series of webinars to demonstrate allied techniques and address common questions, while using a platform like YouTube or Vimeo to share video tutorials and case studies. For more extensive training programs, you could create an interactive online course using a platform like Teachable or Thinkific. So long as everything is connected and relevant, it will help to build your brand!

Remember to track the performance of your educational marketing content across different formats and platforms in the same way as you track all your other content, using metrics such as views, downloads, engagement, and conversions. By implementing these strategies, you will not only improve the user experience but also enhance your aesthetics practice's reputation as a trusted source of valuable information.

CHECKLIST

☑ Use a mix of content formats to appeal to different learning styles.

☑ Keep it simple: Use clear and concise language, avoiding jargon and overly technical terms.

☑ Use real-world examples for good storytelling.

☑ Organize content logically: break down complex ideas into manageable sections.

☑ Include interactive elements like quizzes, polls, or discussion forums to encourage participation.

☑ Provide opportunities for practice and reinforcement: Offer practical exercises, simulations, or work-throughs to help reinforce learning.

☑ Use videos for demonstrations.

☑ E-learning platforms vary widely and require evaluation. Consider also using your website or social media repositories, based on audience reach, functionality and cost.

☑ As always, track content performance.

MARKETING AUTOMATION AND CRM

So far, each chapter has looked at different marketing activities with which you could fill your time, so you could be forgiven for thinking that your entire day belongs to promotion. What if I told you there's a way to:

- streamline your marketing efforts
- save time and resources
- get back time to spend with your family
- and increase your margins
- all without sacrificing engagement with your clients; in fact, being able to provide them with a better experience which will lead to more repeat business?

It's no wonder that my nine-year-old daughter came up with my new favourite word for marketing automation – she calls it "Awesomatic" (she's a smart cookie...)

So in this section, we'll look at the gift that is marketing automation, why it matters, and how it can save you time. Grab a cuppa, put your feet up for once, and let's dive in.

INTRODUCING MARKETING AUTOMATION

Marketing automation refers to the use of technology to automate repetitive marketing tasks, such as emails, social media posts, metrics monitoring and other digital activities. This allows businesses to nurture leads, target their audience more effectively, and manage their marketing campaigns with less manual effort.

76% of companies used marketing automation in 2021.

HTTPS://WWW.HUBSPOT.COM/MARKETING-STATISTICS

Here's why it matters for your practice:

- **Time and Resource Efficiency:** By automating routine tasks, you and your team can focus on more strategic and creative aspects of your marketing plan, resulting in better use of your resources.
- **Enhanced Personalisation:** With marketing automation, you can personalise your messages and offers based on your clients' behaviours and preferences. This ensures that your marketing is more relevant and engaging, leading to higher conversion rates. This is something that only tech can really do – if you try to personalise every email yourself, you'll make mistakes, run out of time or just get bored enough to go bonkers.
- **Improved Customer Experience:** Automated marketing allows you to provide timely and consistent communication with your clients, nurturing their journey from prospect to loyal customer.

The market is flooded with marketing automation tools, each offering different features and capabilities. To help you navigate this landscape, here are a few of the popular marketing automation platforms typically used by services businesses in the UK. All of them offer some sort of free opportunity to nose around, and you should check out what works for you.

But please, just have a look at them for familiarisation purposes – don't even think about buying into any of them until we've looked at your customer workflow (see below).

It's also worth noting that all of them started out as something else (e.g. Mailchimp was originally an email tool) but all of these systems have added automation as part of their key service.

- **HubSpot:** This all-in-one inbound marketing platform offers email marketing, landing pages, social media management, and CRM integration. HubSpot is known for its user-friendly interface and robust analytics, and is probably the #1 choice for enterprise, expanding business marketing. It's also surprisingly cost-effective to get started.
- **Mailchimp:** The popular email marketing tool, Mailchimp also offers marketing automation features, including automated email campaigns, landing pages, and social media scheduling. Mailchimp is an excellent option if you're looking for an affordable, easy-to-use solution focused primarily on email.
- **Marketo:** Now owned by Adobe, Marketo is a comprehensive marketing automation platform that focuses on lead management, email marketing, and campaign optimisation. Marketo is suited to businesses with more complex marketing needs.
- **ActiveCampaign:** This platform combines email marketing, marketing automation, CRM, and sales automation. ActiveCampaign is an excellent choice for small to medium-sized businesses looking to automate their sales and marketing processes.

Now that you know some of the tools available, let's walk through the process of implementing marketing automation.

It's not masses of complex coding. It's not robots. It's not expensive. The suites above are just some of the thousands of simple apps and tools which enable automation. There are also systems that will get these apps to talk to one another whilst you sleep, to ensure that your business processes are happening whether you are at your desk or not. That means your patients can have an enriching and consistent experience with you – the sort that they will tell all their friends about – even when you're at home with the telly on.

And that's the point: automation shouldn't focus on you and your marketing needs first. It should focus on the customer experience whilst saving you time into the bargain. You should map out your client journeys in order to understand the various touchpoints in your clients' interactions with your business, from initial awareness to post-treatment follow-up. How do they discover you? How do they first make contact? What different doors – digital and real – do they come through? This will help you identify the best candidates for automation across the customer experience.

A workflow is a series of automated actions triggered by specific conditions or events. Examples of workflows for an aesthetics practice might include sending a welcome email to new clients who have signed up to a newsletter, scheduling social media posts based on times of the day, or sending appointment reminders one day before an appointment is due. As you can see, workflows can all be described as "when certain conditions are true, do something", or, more succinctly, "if this then that". And that's why, even if you don't use professional automation systems, one of the best small-scale apps for automation is called "IFTTT" – short for "If This Then That". Zapier is another workflow management app worth a look.

Start by automating simple tasks and gradually progress to more complex workflows as you become more comfortable with your platform of choice.

Marketing automation allows you to personalise your messaging based on clients' preferences, behaviours, and interactions with your practice. Use segmentation and dynamic content to create personalised emails, offers, and other communications that resonate with your audience more effectively. Just as you can personalise your emails according to the characteristics of the person (e.g. "Dear Susan" because you know their name), with automation, you can have unlimited exciting gradations of relevance. Imagine automating an offer which opens with "As one of our longest standing clients..." to folks who have been with you for a year or more....

In short, automations achieve two things – they save you time and remove manual labour from annoying and effort-filled activities. But in doing so, they also unlock new forms of activity which you just couldn't do by yourself. And that means your campaigns should become more effective, too. As always, test and optimise them continually and engage in A/B testing (discussed above) to fine-tune your messaging and content – because, with automation, A/B refinements are both economical and informative.

TWENTY TOP AUTOMATIONS TO SAVE YOU TIME AND EFFORT

The best way to explore marketing automation is to actually implement it, so let's explore some of the top automations you can use to save time and effort in your practice. These automations will help you streamline your marketing processes and ensure consistent communication with your clients.

1. **Welcome Emails:** Automatically send a warm and friendly welcome email to new clients, thanking them for choosing your practice and providing essential information about your services.
2. **Appointment Reminders:** Send automated reminders via email and/ or SMS to clients before their appointments, reducing no-shows and improving client satisfaction.

3. **Post-treatment Follow-ups:** Check in with clients after their treatments, asking for feedback and providing aftercare instructions.

4. **Birthday Wishes:** Send personalised birthday messages to your clients, including special offers or discounts as a gift if appropriate.

5. **Newsletter Subscription:** Automatically add new clients to your email list when they sign up online; send them a confirmation email to ensure they're interested in receiving your newsletters.

6. **Review Requests:** Encourage clients to share their experiences by sending automated review requests after their treatments.

7. **Abandoned Cart Recovery:** If you have an e-commerce section on your website, remind clients about items left in their online shopping carts, encouraging them to complete their purchases.

8. **Re-engagement Campaigns:** Target inactive clients with tailored offers and content to encourage them to return to your practice.

9. **Social Media Scheduling:** Automate your social media posts across multiple platforms, ensuring consistent and engaging content for your audience and cutting the time you spend on social posting.

10. **Lead Scoring:** Automatically assign scores to new leads based on their interactions with your practice, helping you identify the most promising prospects.

11. **Drip Campaigns:** Nurture leads through a series of automated, targeted emails, guiding them through the client journey from initial interest to booking an appointment.

12. **Client Segmentation:** Automatically segment your clients based on factors like treatment history, demographics, and preferences to deliver personalised content and offers.

13. **Referral Programs:** Encourage clients to refer friends and family to your practice by automating referral tracking and reward distribution.

14. **Upselling and Cross-selling:** Send targeted recommendations for additional treatments or products that complement your clients' previous purchases.

15. **Treatment Package Reminders:** Notify clients when they have

unused treatments in their package or when their package is about to expire.

16. **Client Milestones:** Celebrate client milestones, such as the anniversary of their first treatment, by sending a personalised message or offer.

17. **Educational Content:** Share valuable information and tips related to aesthetics and skincare with your clients through automated content series.

18. **Promotional Campaigns:** Automate the delivery of special offers, discounts, and seasonal promotions to your clients.

19. **Reporting and Analytics:** Schedule automated reports to help you track the performance of your marketing campaigns and make data-driven decisions.

20. **CRM Integration:** Automatically update your CRM with client information, treatment history, and other relevant data from your marketing automation platform (we'll look at CRM below).

By automating these twenty marketing tasks (and they're only examples – you'll think of many more), you'll not only save time and effort but also create a more personalised and consistent experience for your clients. And the best bit? All of these are "fire and forget" – set them up once and they will deliver value with zero further effort.

CUSTOMER RELATIONSHIP MANAGEMENT (CRM)

In this final section, we'll explore Customer Relationship Management (CRM) – it's a piece of software rather than an automation but delivers similar improvements in marketing effectiveness.

CRM allows businesses to manage and analyse their interactions with clients and prospects. A CRM system enables you to organise, track, and streamline client information, helping you build and maintain strong relationships with your clients, as well as identify potential new clients.

In short, CRM helps you get to know your clients better, improving communication and enhancing their overall experience with your aesthetics practice. That's the official description. In reality, for a small business, it means basic record-keeping so that you don't lose track of where you are with each client. If you have 500 clients on your books, it's the place to note what treatments a client has had, when, what they are interested in, what they think of your practice and anything else which will allow you to engage with them in a more meaningful way.

Of course, as we've seen above, the big marketing and sales platforms (Marketo, HubSpot, Mailchimp, etc.) are all merging bits of functionality, so they're all doing a bit of CRM too. You may therefore find that you've already got some CRM tools. If not, as well as the big names in CRM (Salesforce, Pipedrive, Sugar, Insightly), there are hundreds of cheap and even free options. Here's what they'll give you:

- **Centralised Client Information:** A single, centralised platform for storing all your client data, making it easily accessible to your entire team.
- **Improved Client Communication:** By keeping a record of all your interactions with clients, CRM ensures that your team has access to the most up-to-date information, making personalised, relevant and efficient communication a pushover.
- **Enhanced Client Retention:** By tracking client interactions, preferences, and treatment history, CRM means you can anticipate and address your clients' needs, leading to increased satisfaction and loyalty (and ideally more income too – imagine being able to point out to a client that they're due for a follow-up: it's the perfect sell...)
- **Better Time Management:** CRM systems streamline your workflow, helping anyone involved in sales stay organised and focused on their tasks. If, like many aestheticians, you're fundamentally a one-person practice, this is significant. You need to be doing, not selling. So CRM is actually more useful for small businesses, not less so.

CRM really is the most overheated market in tech. There is no way we can legitimately recommend the right CRM system to you because there are so many, however, here's the list of recommended platforms for smaller businesses from startups.co.uk in February 2023, with their roots too (remember we saw above that most CRMs today are offshoots of other types of software):

What?	From where?	Why?
Hubspot	Email marketing	Superb free plan. Nobody gives you more for nothing
Monday.com	Project Management	Great management dashboards, seriously flexible
Freshsales	CRM from the ground up	Easy to use with a super-simple setup and full of handy tools like lead-scoring
Zoho	A bit of everything	Tons of features, hugely extensible
Pipedrive	CRM from the ground up	Brilliant contact management
Zendesk	Customer service/support	Excellent support system

Do make sure that your CRM system complies with data protection regulations, such as the General Data Protection Regulation (GDPR); most systems sold in the UK are fully compliant, but there are lesser-known brands elsewhere in the world which definitely aren't. As your practice grows, your CRM system should be able to accommodate your expanding needs, so choose a CRM solution that offers scalability and flexibility for future growth. All of the above options will comfortably grow with you. Some of the smaller platforms (especially ones which bolt onto your own email) won't grow well.

Perhaps more important now than ever before, go for a CRM system that allows you to customise its features and interface to suit your practice's specific requirements. With so much functionality, being easy to use, customisable to your workflows and able to deliver value in lots of ways to everyone on your team might be the most important factor in your choice.

Whichever you go for, keep your data carefully organised. Make sure that all client information is entered and updated consistently across your team. Beware of errors and inconsistencies – nobody likes people getting their name wrong! CRM abides by the rule "rubbish in, rubbish out": if the information you store isn't right, then the service you provide won't be right either. The data you keep needs to be complete, consistent and carefully maintained. In terms of completeness, consider including:

- **Contact Information:** Name, email address, phone number, and other relevant contact details.
- **Demographics:** Age, gender, location, and other pertinent demographic information.
- **Treatment History:** A record of all treatments the client has received, including dates, practitioners, and outcomes.
- **Preferences and Interests:** Information about your clients' preferences, such as favourite treatments, skin type, and preferred communication methods.
- **Client Feedback:** Notes and insights from client feedback, including testimonials, reviews, and survey responses. If you have to copy reviews from other sites, that's worth your time!
- **Interaction History:** Records of all communication and interactions with the client, including emails, phone calls, and in-person appointments.
- **Marketing Data:** Details about the client's engagement with your marketing campaigns, such as email opens, clicks, and website visits.

It's everyone's job to maintain this data (even though it's boring!), so provide your team with comprehensive training on how to use your CRM system effectively. Just like every other aspect of customer service, you're only as good as your worst interaction with the customer, so everyone on your team needs to be CRM-savvy.

With all that effort and data management, you'll want the best return for your input. So, to maximise efficiency, integrate your CRM system with other tools you use, such as marketing automation platforms, appointment scheduling software, and financial systems. You won't just save time and effort (see the automations covered in the previous section), you'll also provide a more consistent level of service. Think about:

- **Personalisation:** Use the data stored in your CRM to personalise your marketing messages, tailoring content and offers based on your clients' preferences, history, and behaviours.
- **Segmentation:** Group your clients into segments based on their characteristics and behaviours, allowing you to create targeted marketing campaigns that hit home with specific audiences.
- **Lead Nurturing:** Use the information in your CRM to create targeted, automated marketing campaigns that guide prospects through the client journey, from initial interest to booking an appointment.
- **Analytics and Reporting:** Use the data and insights from your CRM to measure the performance of your marketing campaigns and in particular to understand why a campaign might or might not have worked.
- **Multi-channel Marketing:** Your CRM data can help you determine which marketing channels (e.g., email, social media, or paid advertising) are most effective for engaging with specific client segments, allowing you to allocate your resources more strategically.

A HOLISTIC AUTOMATION STRATEGY

By now, it should be clear that CRM is a valuable component of practice management as well as marketing. Managing clients on your mobile phone, on a notepad, or in your head is no longer an option! On my coaching calls, when I ask, "Are you still using a paper diary?", if the client answers yes, I push the big red button and the trapdoor opens...

But that doesn't mean that CRM is the be-all and end-all. Provided we take our cue carefully from the patient journey, we can look at multiple elements of digitisation and automation which will not only create efficiency in the business, free up new time to treat more patients and make more money, but also maintain a fantastic experience for our patients. This can be the key to scaling the business by ensuring we never lose a good patient yet find time to attract new ones. My automation strategy features eight elements:

- **Online booking:** As I said above, if you're using paper for bookings, you're wasting time and sacrificing service into the bargain. Any major website system (WordPress, Squarespace) will include off-the-shelf booking systems which you can switch on in minutes. I think clinics should offer two paths into this booking system via their website. For new/potential patients, you will typically want them to book a consultation and to feel unpressured. It's an exploratory discussion. I would therefore suggest removing all other options from your initial booking form for new patients. I think it can be both confusing and inefficient for a new patient to be confronted with a full list of treatments. It's also a waste of time for them to randomly book these treatments without prior consultation – you then have to call them back, fix up a consultation instead, etc. What a waste of effort! I therefore advise that the marketing side of your website should just focus on creating a seamless journey towards booking an initial consultation online. Everything else can wait – and can feel like exclusive access to the full list of treatments!
- **Payments:** We're not going to have a business without money, so a great booking system will also feature integrated payments using respected third-party services like Stripe. You might think that demanding payment upfront is asking too much, but rest assured,

we're all used to paying upfront for services. Don't bother with taking a deposit – take the full fee: it will reduce no-shows, and that instantly improves your profitability. No-shows are the worst booking outcome because it's money you can't get back (unless you're blessed with a very convenient walk-in off the street…) As well as card payment systems, consider using a system like GoCardless too. GoCardless allows you to easily create Direct Debits for patients who want to sign up for long-term treatment plans or subscriptions (and if you haven't got long-term plans, you're really missing out on easy money!) Again, payments are no longer a hurdle to patient participation; they improve the patient experience by being convenient, fast, and mobile-friendly.

■ **Accounting:** Provided you have a good digital accounting system (Xero, QuickBooks, etc.), a modern payment system will enable you to automate many tasks relating to finance and bookkeeping. For example, if you use Xero for accounting, and any clinic management / CRM software that integrates with Zapier (as we saw above), then you can easily create a workflow that will automatically generate invoices for every booking made, meaning all your accounting can be done to a compliant standard without you having to lift a finger! Systems like Xero will also automatically chase up any pesky unpaid invoices on your behalf by sending personalised email reminders for outstanding payments at set intervals of your choice.

■ **Reminders:** We talked about no-shows earlier; it's essential to send reminders to patients – and ideally, we'll repeat the process for pre-care and aftercare around the appointment. Good booking systems will allow you to create several automated engagements to make life easier for both you and your patient:

☐ Put the appointment in your calendar.
☐ Send an email or digital nudge to put the appointment in the patient's calendar (I am fond of Calendly for this purpose).

☐ Create and configure automated reminders with information about the upcoming appointment, your clinic's location, any preparation you expect the patient to do, and links to paperwork, etc., that they might need before the appointment day.

These automated messages can now take the form of email, SMS or even WhatsApp messages that are personalised, timely and most importantly automatic, saving you countless hours of repetitive tasks which would frankly be impossible if conducted manually. These reminders create a more caring and patient-centric service which your patients will respect, and which improves their perception of your business – all while reducing expensive no-shows!

■ **Compliance:** Of course, it's non-negotiable that your clinic keeps compliant, accurate and secure patient records. And that's something which is increasingly hard to do with paper records. A good clinical management platform will include:

☐ **GDPR compliance,** including explicit consent for communications and marketing emails so you can build a legitimate mailing list of patients.

☐ **Consent:** the ability to create your own online forms for detailing consent or sign-up information for example.

☐ **Repositories** for detailed and secure patient notes, including logging details of previous treatments, stock used, future treatment plans, etc.

☐ **Security by default.** If it's a US-built software, look out for the HIPAA certificate. If it's from the UK, ask for equivalent credentials in data security.

This isn't just about the platform – we're looking for opportunities to automate your effort out of the equation, so, use the platform to ensure you stay compliant by getting signatures and permissions where you need them in the patient journey without having to remember to ask for them yourself.

That's five opportunities for automation. The other three are intricately interrelated: The ability to:

- **segment** your own data, e.g. by treatment type, condition, age, location, spend or last treatment date, so that you can send hyper-targeted and therefore very timely marketing communications. For example, a great system will allow you to write a workflow that checks on a daily basis for men who had a filler treatment more than 4 months ago. It will then send those men a targeted, personalised email, offering useful information about filler treatments for men and the aftercare which might interest them, and, of course, how to get booked back in for a follow-up consultation.
- create regular and automated **email marketing**. This is to drive retention of your existing patients, attract new business via referrals and reviews, and create new value via upsell opportunities.
- build pre-programmed **workflows of communications**, across multiple channels, that are triggered by certain events. For example, the act of booking a consultation can also "subscribe" that patient to a series of emails and WhatsApp messages over a period of time covering both before and after the appointment. They will feature a combination of practical information, educational information, and promotion of related treatments, requests for referrals and Google reviews, etc.

There is no limit to the sophistication of these workflows – you can even introduce layers and logic to them; for example, assessing whether a client has bought multiple products, changing communications according to their sentiment (e.g. have they left a bad review?!). I often create workflows across a whole year – including sending patients a "happy birthday" message!

As I've said before, these levels of engagement aren't really even possible without automation. Try writing an email by hand to even five people and I guarantee you'll mess it up by calling someone the wrong name because you copied and pasted it from the previous email! We've all done it. Serious engagement demands automation, and with data segmentation, scripts and workflows in place, your clinic's system can become a communications and marketing machine that saves you thousands of hours, while upping your revenue and retention rates too. And that means you can scale your business without driving yourself or your team to exhaustion.

CHECKLIST

☑ Explore popular marketing automation and CRM platforms to find the best fit for your practice.

☑ Map out your client journeys to identify candidates for automation.

☑ Create and implement workflows to automate tasks, such as sending welcome emails, scheduling social media posts, or sending appointment reminders.

☑ Gradually progress from automating simple tasks to more complex workflows as you become more comfortable with your chosen platform.

☑ Use automation to deliver new techniques, e.g. personalisations.

☑ Optimize and A/B-test to refine your marketing automation campaigns.

☑ Ensure your CRM system is consistently and accurately maintained. In CRM, data is everything.

☑ Integrate your CRM system with other tools and platforms (e.g. appointment scheduling, financial systems, etc.).

ANALYTICS & DECISION-MAKING

In every chapter so far, we've looked at ways of marketing your aesthetics practice. And every chapter has also finished with the cautionary tale that, to ensure your marketing efforts align with your practice's objectives and budgets, it's essential to measure and monitor your marketing activities. And for most types of marketing activity, we've recommended Key Performance Indicators (KPIs) to help you understand that particular mechanism.

The KPIs for each marketing tool do vary a little, but there are some general rules of thumb. If you can measure it, you should. Because if you can measure it, you can understand it, and do something about it if things are looking dicey. So, in this chapter, we'll take a whistlestop tour of analytics in general.

87% of marketers say data is their company's most under-utilised asset.

HTTPS://WWW.INVOCA.COM/BLOG/STATE-OF-DATA-
DRIVEN-MARKETING-UPDATE-YOUR-STRATEGY

KPIs are measurable values that show how effectively your marketing initiatives are achieving your business goals. By tracking the right KPIs, you can make data-driven decisions to optimize your marketing strategy and improve your practice's performance. Here are ten top marketing KPIs:

TEN TOP KPIS FOR YOUR PRACTICE

Customer Acquisition Cost (CAC)

CAC is the total cost of acquiring a new customer, including marketing expenses, salaries, and other related expenses. It's essential to know your CAC to evaluate the effectiveness of your marketing campaigns and ensure you're spending your resources wisely.

To calculate CAC, divide your total marketing expenses by the number of new customers acquired during a specific period.

Let's say you want to calculate your Customer Acquisition Cost (CAC) for the month of January. Here's a breakdown of your marketing expenses for that month:

Online advertising: £2,000
Print advertising: £1,000
Social media marketing: £500
Email marketing: £300
Total marketing expenses = £2,000 + £1,000 + £500 + £300 = £3,800

Now, let's assume that during January, your aesthetics practice acquired 20 new customers.

To calculate CAC, divide your total marketing expenses by the number of new customers:

$$CAC = £3,800 / 20 = £190$$

In this example, your Customer Acquisition Cost for January is £190. This means that, on average, you spent £190 to acquire each new customer during that month.

Customer Lifetime Value (CLV)

CLV is an estimation of the total revenue a customer will generate for your aesthetics practice throughout their entire relationship with your business. By comparing CLV with CAC, you can determine whether your marketing investments are paying off in the long run.

To calculate CLV, multiply the average revenue per customer by the average customer lifespan (in years) and subtract the initial CAC.

Suppose you want to calculate the Customer Lifetime Value (CLV) for your aesthetics practice. First, you'll need to gather the following data:

Average revenue per customer: This is the average amount a customer spends at your practice. Let's say your customers, on average, spend £500 per year.

Average customer lifespan: This is the average length of time a customer continues to do business with your practice. Let's assume that, on average, customers remain loyal to your practice for 3 years.

Initial Customer Acquisition Cost (CAC): This is the cost of acquiring a new customer, which we calculated in the previous example as £190.

Now, you can calculate the CLV using the formula:

CLV = (Average revenue per customer x Average customer lifespan) –
Initial CAC
CLV = (£500 x 3) – £190
CLV = £1,500 – £190
CLV = £1,310

In this example, your Customer Lifetime Value is £1,310. This means that, on average, each customer generates £1,310 in revenue for your practice over their entire relationship with your business, after accounting for the initial cost of acquiring them.

Conversion Rate

The conversion rate is the percentage of prospects who take a desired action, such as booking a consultation or making a purchase. By tracking conversion rates for different marketing activities, you can determine which tactics are most effective and allocate resources accordingly.

To calculate the conversion rate, divide the number of successful conversions by the total number of prospects and multiply by 100.

Consider the example where you want to calculate the conversion rate for a specific marketing campaign aimed at getting new clients to book a consultation at your aesthetics practice. Here's the data you'll need:

Successful conversions: This refers to the number of prospects who took the desired action as a result of your marketing campaign. Let's say 40 people booked a consultation.

Total number of prospects: This is the total number of people who were exposed to your marketing campaign. Let's assume 400 prospects received your promotional email or saw your online ad.

Now, you can calculate the conversion rate using the formula:

Conversion Rate = (Number of successful conversions / Total number of prospects) x 100

Conversion Rate = (40 / 400) x 100
Conversion Rate = 0.1 x 100
Conversion Rate = 10%

In this example, your marketing campaign's conversion rate is 10%. This means that 10% of the prospects who were exposed to your campaign took the desired action of booking a consultation.

Click-Through Rate (CTR)

CTR is the percentage of people who click on a specific link, such as an ad or a call-to-action button in an email. It helps you understand how engaging your marketing materials are and whether your audience finds them relevant and valuable.

To calculate CTR, divide the total number of clicks by the total number of impressions (times the link was shown) and multiply by 100.

Let's say you want to calculate the Click-Through Rate (CTR) for an online ad campaign promoting a new treatment at your aesthetics practice. Here's the data you'll need:

Total number of clicks: This is the number of times users clicked on your ad. Let's say your ad received 80 clicks.

Total number of impressions: This is the number of times your ad was shown to users. Let's assume your ad had 2,000 impressions.

Now, you can calculate the CTR using the formula:

CTR = (Total number of clicks / Total number of impressions) x 100
CTR = (80 / 2,000) x 100
CTR = 0.04 x 100
CTR = 4%

In this example, your online ad campaign's Click-Through Rate is 4%. This means that out of the 2,000 times your ad was shown, users clicked on it 80 times, resulting in a 4% CTR.

Cost per Click (CPC)

CPC is the average cost you pay for each click on your digital ads. Monitoring CPC helps you manage your advertising budget and evaluate the effectiveness of your ad campaigns.

To calculate CPC, divide the total cost of the ad campaign by the total number of clicks received.

In this example, you want to calculate the Cost per Click (CPC) for an online ad campaign promoting a new treatment. Here's the data you'll need:

Total cost of the ad campaign: This is the amount you spent on the campaign. Let's say you spent £800 on this campaign.

Total number of clicks: This is the number of times users clicked on your ad. Let's assume your ad received 200 clicks.

Now, you can calculate the CPC using the formula:

CPC = Total cost of the ad campaign / Total number of clicks
CPC = £800 / 200
CPC = £4

In this example, your online ad campaign's Cost per Click is £4. This means that, on average, you paid £4 for each click on your ad.

Return on Advertising Spend (ROAS)

ROAS measures the revenue generated from your advertising campaigns relative to the amount spent. It helps you determine the effectiveness of your ad spend and make informed decisions about your advertising strategy.

To calculate ROAS, divide the total revenue generated by the ad campaign by the total ad spend.

Suppose you want to calculate the Return on Advertising Spend (ROAS) for an online ad campaign. Here's the data you'll need:

Total revenue generated by the ad campaign: This is the amount of money your business made as a direct result of the campaign. Let's say the new treatment bookings from this campaign generated £6,000 in revenue.

Total ad spend: This is the amount you spent on the ad campaign. Let's assume you spent £1,200 on this campaign.

Now, you can calculate the ROAS using the formula:

ROAS = Total revenue generated by the ad campaign / Total ad spend
ROAS = £6,000 / £1,200
ROAS = 5

In this example, your online ad campaign's Return on Advertising Spend is 5. This means that for every £1 spent on the ad campaign, your business generated £5 in revenue. A higher ROAS indicates that your ad campaign is generating more revenue relative to its cost, which is a positive sign for your marketing efforts.

Email Open Rate

The email open rate is the percentage of recipients who open your emails. A high open rate indicates that your subject lines and sender information are compelling and relevant to your audience.

To calculate the email open rate, divide the total number of opened emails by the total number of delivered emails and multiply by 100.

Social Media Engagement Rate

The social media engagement rate is a measure of how actively your audience interacts with your content on social platforms. It helps you understand the effectiveness of your social media marketing efforts and identify the types of content that resonate with your audience.

To calculate engagement rate, divide the total number of likes, comments, and shares by the total number of followers and multiply by 100.

Website Bounce Rate

The bounce rate is the percentage of website visitors who leave your site after viewing only one page. A high bounce rate may indicate that your website's content, layout, or user experience isn't meeting the expectations of your visitors. Monitoring bounce rate can help you identify areas for improvement and create a more engaging online experience for your audience.

To calculate the bounce rate, divide the total number of single-page sessions by the total number of sessions and multiply by 100.

Net Promoter Score (NPS)

NPS is a measure of customer satisfaction and loyalty. It's based on the question: "How likely are you to recommend our aesthetics practice to a friend or colleague?" Respondents rate their likelihood on a scale of 0 to 10, with 0 being "not at all likely" and 10 being "extremely likely." NPS can help you understand the overall satisfaction of your clients and identify opportunities for improvement.

To calculate NPS, subtract the percentage of detractors (those who rate your practice 0-6) from the percentage of promoters (those who rate your practice 9-10).

Here's a walkthrough. You've surveyed your clients and asked them to rate their likelihood of recommending your practice to a friend or colleague on a scale of 0 to 10. Here's the data you've collected:

Total number of respondents: 100

Number of promoters (those who rated your practice 9-10): 60

Number of detractors (those who rated your practice 0-6): 20

First, you'll need to calculate the percentage of promoters and detractors.

Percentage of promoters = (Number of promoters / Total number of respondents) x 100

Percentage of promoters = (60 / 100) x 100 = 60%

Percentage of detractors = (Number of detractors / Total number of respondents) x 100

Percentage of detractors = (20 / 100) x 100 = 20%

Now, you can calculate the NPS using the formula:

NPS = Percentage of promoters – Percentage of detractors

NPS = 60% – 20%

NPS = 40

In this example, your aesthetics practice's Net Promoter Score is 40. This indicates that, overall, your clients are more likely to recommend your practice than not. NPS can range from –100 (all detractors) to 100 (all promoters), so a score of 40 is considered good.

Obtaining this data will involve using tools like Google Analytics, social media platforms' built-in analytics, email marketing software, and customer relationship management (CRM) systems to cobble data together, but once you've set it all up, the data will flow without too much further effort.

There are plenty more KPIs which you can choose to use to measure your marketing performance. Similarly, some of these may be too much hassle or not worth your interest. Experience will tell you what best reflects profitability in your business, but whatever floats your boat, now that you're familiar with the essential marketing KPIs and how a bit of analysis can help you make sense of the data, you can start monitoring them to gain valuable insights into your marketing efforts.

In the next section, we'll dive deeper into how to analyze and interpret marketing data to make data-driven decisions and optimize your marketing strategy.

DO SOMETHING USEFUL WITH YOUR DATA!

In the previous section, we discussed the importance of understanding key performance indicators (KPIs) to track and measure your marketing efforts. That's great in principle, but we still need to get the raw data and put it to work.

"In God we trust; all others must bring data."

W. EDWARDS DEMING, STATISTICIAN AND MANAGEMENT CONSULTANT.

The annoying thing is that your data will be in an increasing number of different sources. Web analytics tools like Google Analytics or your own website logs will provide insights into your website's performance, user behaviour and traffic sources. Each social media platform will have its own built-in analytics tools to help you track engagement, reach, and conversion metrics for your content and campaigns. Your email marketing software will provide data on email open rates, click-through rates, and conversions. And if you have a CRM system, there will be classes of data in there too, including demographic information, purchase history, and interactions with your brand.

Exactly what that looks like will depend on your setup. What we can say is that marshalling data is an absolute pain, and anything you can do to schedule and automate its analysis will be useful. Big businesses have data analysts who do this sort of thing every day of the week but you can't afford that. So find ways to schedule the extraction of key headline figures from the torrent of raw data, and to do so regularly enough and in a way that is easy enough to interpret so that you can get on with running the business.

To make sense of your data:

- **Identify trends and patterns:** Look for trends in your data that may indicate areas of success or opportunities for improvement. This includes identifying which marketing channels generate the most leads, which campaigns have the highest conversion rates, or which treatments have the highest customer satisfaction ratings.
- **Segment your data:** Break your data down into smaller, more specific groups to gain deeper insights. For example, you can segment your data by customer demographics, marketing channels, or customer lifetime value. This will help you tailor your marketing efforts to better target specific audiences and improve overall effectiveness. That said, don't slice and dice your data too much. A few big segments are a good representation of your market. Lots of small segments just means you'll end up pandering to every last little group and miss the bigger, more important trends.
- **Use visualizations:** Visualizing your data using charts and graphs can make it easier to identify trends, patterns, and outliers. Tools like Microsoft Excel, Google Sheets, or specialized data visualization software can help you create meaningful visualizations that aid in data interpretation. Tableau and FusionCharts are a good place to start.

Finally, put your data to work to improve your marketing outcomes (or the whole thing has been rather pointless!) Use your data to:

- **Test and optimize:** Continuously test new marketing ideas, track their performance, and adjust your strategy based on the results. This iterative approach helps you identify the most effective tactics and maximize your marketing ROI without taking big risks.

- **Allocate resources more effectively:** By understanding which marketing channels, campaigns, or activities yield the best results, you can allocate your budget and resources more efficiently.
- **Tailor your messaging:** Use insights from customer segments and preferences to create more targeted and personalized marketing messages that resonate with your audience.
- There are also some do's and don'ts to consider. In fact, they really are just don'ts....
- **Don't just rely on quantitative (numeric) data:** While this data is crucial, don't overlook the importance of qualitative (conversational) data, such as customer feedback and testimonials. Qualitative data can provide valuable context and insights that quantitative data alone may not reveal. Quantitative data will give you the "what" of your marketing, while qualitative data will give you the "why".
- **Don't forget your data privacy obligations:** Comply with data privacy regulations and respect your clients' privacy when collecting, storing, and analysing data – don't forget that plenty of customer data is identifiable and can lead to intensely personal analytics.
- **Don't ignore context:** When analyzing data, always consider the context in which it was collected. External factors, such as seasonal trends or market changes, can impact your data and should be taken into account when making decisions.
- **Don't fall into the trap of confirmation bias:** Avoid using data selectively to confirm your pre-existing beliefs. Instead, approach your analysis with an open mind and be willing to revise your assumptions based on the insights you discover.

In fact, there's always a conflict between data-powered decisions, gut instinct, and the biases which challenge both ways of making decisions. Don't discount the value of intuition and experience – it's where some of the most creative approaches come from. Use data as a starting point, but add other factors – your professional experience, industry trends, and input from friends and colleagues – before making a final decision on a new marketing activity. And in the absence of data, absolutely trust your intuition – it'll almost certainly be right.

CHECKLIST

☑ Metrics are the lifeblood of good decision-making. Use all available data to make informed marketing decisions.

☑ Identify trends and patterns in your data to find areas of success and opportunities for improvement.

☑ Regularly iterate your marketing tactics based on data-driven insights (and a dose of instinct).

☑ Don't rely solely on quantitative data.

☑ Be sure to comply with data privacy regulations.

KEEP IN TOUCH WITH YOUR CUSTOMERS

You've undoubtedly seen your fair share of clients coming through your doors. Whether they're there for a quick touch-up or a more involved treatment, the key to your practice's success lies in not only attracting new clients but also maintaining and nurturing relationships with your existing ones.

And that's a good plan: studies have shown that it costs five times more to acquire a new client than to retain an existing one. Moreover, your existing clients are more likely to try new services and recommend your practice to friends and family, leading to a steady stream of new clients through word-of-mouth marketing.

Client retention is also directly linked to profitability. According to a study by Bain & Company[1], a 5% increase in client retention can lead to a 25% to 95% increase in profits. These statistics highlight the cost-effectiveness of focusing on client retention versus acquisition, and the undeniable benefits of investing in strategies to maintain relationships with your current clients.

---

1   "Prescription for Cutting Costs," and it was conducted by Frederick F. Reichheld and W. Earl Sasser, Jr. 1990

A STRATEGY FOR CLIENT COMMUNICATION

A well-crafted client communication strategy is your starting point for building and maintaining strong relationships with your clients, and understanding their needs, preferences, and expectations is the starting point in putting together the plan. Client surveys are an invaluable tool for collecting this information. They can help you understand what clients value most about your services and uncover trends that can inform your marketing decisions.

Use a mix of open-ended and closed-ended questions in your surveys. Open-ended questions allow clients to express their thoughts freely, while closed-ended questions can provide quantitative data for analysis. Topics to cover in a survey include:

- Overall satisfaction with your services
- Satisfaction with specific treatments or products
- Communication preferences (e.g., email, phone, text)
- Desired frequency of communication
- Areas for improvement or suggestions for new services

When conducting surveys, remember to respect your clients' time. Keep the survey brief, and consider offering an incentive, such as a discount on their next treatment, to encourage participation. Most of us will get these surveys by email, but it's also worth using a feedback form to grab customers immediately after a successful procedure.

"Desired frequency of communication" is a crucial question. Striking the right balance between frequency and relevance is important to maintaining client engagement without overwhelming. Too much com-munication can lead to "communication fatigue," causing clients to tune out or, worse, unsubscribe altogether. On the other hand, too little com-munication can result in clients feeling neglected or forgotten. The sweet spot is somewhere in between.

Monitor your clients' engagement with your communications, such as open rates for emails and click-through rates for social media posts. If you notice a decline in engagement, consider adjusting the frequency or content of your communications. Remember, it's better to send fewer, more relevant messages than to bombard clients with information they may not find valuable, or which is just too salesy.

Repeat customers have been measured to spend an average of 67% more than new customers.

HTTPS://WWW.THINKIMPACT.COM/CUSTOMER-RETENTION-STATISTICS

Better still, stay relevant with some personalisation. Start by addressing your clients by their first name in emails, text messages, and other communications. This simple gesture creates a sense of familiarity and connection. Next, use the information you've gathered through client surveys and segmentation to tailor your content to clients' interests and preferences. For example, you might send targeted emails promoting specific treatments only to those clients who have expressed interest in those services; or share blog posts and articles relevant to their concerns and goals.

Asking about "communication preferences" is also helpful. Leveraging multiple communication channels allows you to reach your clients where they are most comfortable and engaged (see below). Equally, don't commit to only using their channels of choice – you'll be cutting off some useful and even respected ways of reaching them. A patient might instinctively only check the "email" box – and yet would actually be very happy to get an appointment reminder by text message.

Finally, as part of your plan, be sure to track and measure its impact. Monitor key performance indicators (KPIs) such as open rates, click-through rates, response rates, and conversion rates to assess the success of your work. Be open to experimentation and don't be afraid to make adjustments to your strategy as needed.

SAME CHANNELS, DIFFERENT STYLE

Most of your original news today will have come from the web. There are far more channels for existing client engagement, though. An effective client communication strategy relies on using a diverse mix of channels to maintain and enhance those relationships. Here are some of the ideas to drop into the mix:

Email Newsletters and Updates

Pretty much the most versatile and effective tool for staying connected with your clients. They provide an opportunity to share important updates, promotions, educational content, and more, directly to your clients' inboxes. We cover all the themes for good emails in more depth in Chapter 6 (email marketing), but remember that email newsletters succeed on:

- **Subject lines** that pique curiosity, especially if they're personalised
- **Design** that's clean and easy to read on both desktop and mobile devices
- **Content** that caters to different client interests, features appropriate promotions and has clear headings to make it easy for clients to skim through
- Clear **calls to action (CTAs)** that guide clients toward their next steps, such as booking an appointment, redeeming a special offer, or reading a blog post.

Social Media Engagement and Private Messaging

Social media platforms give you real-time engagement with your clients. We cover marketing on social media in Chapter 6, but now we're talking about engaging with people we already know, and that means engagement, not content creation. Be responsive to comments and messages on your social media channels. Give prompt, thoughtful replies which demonstrate that you value your clients' input. Also, participate on their social media if you have something useful, advisory, or just plain friendly to say.

Most social media platforms provide private messaging options too, which enable you to engage with existing clients in a more personal and direct manner. Use these features to answer questions, address concerns, or share exclusive offers.

SMS and Mobile App Notifications

Text messages and mobile app notifications are a powerful way to deliver timely, relevant and short information directly to your clients' smartphones. As with all media, always obtain explicit consent from clients before sending them text messages or app notifications (through sign-up forms, client surveys, or during the initial consultation). People are especially sensitive about intrusion by phone, so stay on the right side of the law!

Also, because SMS and app notifications interrupt the recipient, be mindful of the timing of your messages. Avoid sending messages too early or too late in the day and consider scheduling messages to arrive during times when clients are most likely to be receptive. It's often helpful to send emails at 3 am. It's never helpful to send an app marketing notification at 3 am!

Keep SMS messages short, relevant and to the point – they'll be better received and are easier to produce, too! Use clear, concise language, and avoid using industry jargon that clients may not understand. Appointment reminders, special promotions, and important updates are all appropriate for SMS and app notifications and will usually be gratefully received as a helpful part of the service. Avoid sending too many promotional messages, which may be perceived as spam.

Even with SMS, there still needs to be an easy way to unsubscribe. Provide a clear and easy way for clients to opt out of receiving future text messages or app notifications.

Direct Mail and Physical Touchpoints

Don't forget the real world! Although digital channels have become increasingly popular, direct mail and physical touchpoints also belong in your strategy. In fact, it's so rare that people bother with real-world effort that it can sometimes be a delightful differentiator!

Treat direct mail exactly like emails: personalise them, send them to selected recipients if you can, and time campaigns strategically – considering factors such as seasonality, holidays, and local events. For example, sending a holiday card or a summer skincare promotion can be particularly effective.

Far more than is the case with emails, design is a chance to stand out – or fail. Would you trust a flyer for an aesthetics practice which came through your door looking like the menu from the local Chinese takeaway? Nope! Invest in high-quality, visually appealing designs that reflect your brand's image and values; and use a quality finish or creative to really stand out from the millions of emails we all suffer with daily.

Real and Virtual Client Appreciation Events

Client appreciation events are an excellent way to show your gratitude for your clients' support and loyalty. These events can be held in person or virtually, depending on your clients' preferences and, of course, our current public health guidelines. Events can be educational workshops, product demonstrations, treatment giveaways, or just a simple party with some drinks and snacks. Virtual events can be held through platforms like Zoom, Facebook Live, or Instagram Live (great for educational activities – not so great for drinks and snacks). What really works here is the sense of exclusivity: you're holding an event just for the select people who count themselves lucky enough to be your clients! So use your usual direct channels to promote the event and generate excitement. Send personalized invitations, create eye-catching social media posts and make them sparkle! Don't sell – at least, not too much. You're there to show appreciation; express your gratitude to clients for their support and loyalty and sow the seeds of future business. By all means, offer exclusive discounts, giveaways, or special offers as a token of appreciation, but don't make it a hard sell! After the event, send a follow-up email or message to thank attendees for their participation, and again, keep it positive, optimistic and human.

97% of B2B marketers believe that in-person events have a major impact on achieving business outcomes.

HTTPS://WWW.BIZZABO.COM/BLOG/EVENT-MARKETING-STATISTICS BIZZABO 2019

Loyalty programmes

There's one form of engagement which only comes into play with existing clients. Loyalty programs are a powerful tool for retaining clients, driving repeat business, and encouraging referrals. A well-designed loyalty program rewards clients for their continued patronage and incentivizes them to return to your practice while not being too salesy or too costly to operate. The key components are:

- **Simplicity:** Ensure your loyalty program is easy to understand and participate in. Clients are more likely to engage with a program that has clear, straightforward rules and rewards, which they can make a start on easily. Think of your coffee shop loyalty card!
- **Personalization:** Tailor your loyalty program to suit the unique needs and preferences of your clients. Use the data you've gathered through surveys and segmentation to offer rewards and incentives that align with clients' interests and treatment history.
- **Flexibility:** Offer a range of rewards and redemption options to accommodate clients with different preferences and spending habits. This could include discounts on treatments, free products, or priority booking for appointments.
- **Communication:** Keep clients informed about their progress in your loyalty program through regular updates and reminders. Use your communication channels to highlight the benefits of your program and encourage clients to work towards their next reward.

Do check out the other chapters here which look at individual marketing techniques and employ them for client retention too. Just remember that on the one hand, you need to be more considerate than ever – because these are people who have already given you money. On the other, you can meet their needs more effectively – also because these are people who have already given you money! In particular, also check out Chapter 11 – Managing your online reputation. It deals with an important piece of engagement with your existing customers: referrals, reviews and word-of-mouth marketing.

CHECKLIST

☑ Craft a well-rounded client communication strategy to stay in touch with customers.

☑ Use multiple communication channels, including email newsletters, social media, SMS and app notifications and events.

☑ Give emails attention-grabbing subject lines and relevant content with clear calls to action.

☑ Be responsive and engaging on social media channels.

☑ Organize real and virtual client appreciation events to show gratitude and strengthen relationships with your customers.

☑ Consider a simple loyalty program.

BRIDGING THE GAP – DIGITAL AND PHYSICAL

We live in changing times. What used to be physical is now digital. But have we lost sight of the human touch in our marketing? Since aesthetics is a hands-on and intensely personal experience, it would be a shame if the digital experience – which might be the first touchpoint a customer has with your practice – is dramatically different from the physical experience.

According to a survey by Retail Dive, 87% of customers say they want a consistent experience across all channels, including in-store and online. Your brand needs to be consistent and cohesive. Everything must hang together.

Creating a unified marketing approach helps to establish trust and credibility with potential clients, making it easier for them to navigate the customer journey from initial online touchpoints, such as websites, social media, and email marketing, to the physical experience of visiting a practice.

Some of this is about branding – ensuring that what you do online matches the look, feel and image of your physical practice. Increasingly, however, there is a world of digital tools which connect with and influence the physical world. Some cost only pennies while others are an expensive glimpse into a very different future. But all are exciting tools which will bring our real and digital worlds together. In the following sections, we will explore some of the tools and techniques for bridging the digital and physical divide, creating a cohesive brand experience across your marketing channels.

TOOLS AND TECHNIQUES – INTEGRATING DIGITAL AND PHYSICAL MARKETING

In this section, we will explore four key tools and techniques that can be used to effectively link digital and physical marketing in the aesthetics industry in a meaningful way: QR codes, Augmented Reality (AR), Near Field Communication (NFC), and geofencing.

QR Codes

Quick Response (QR) codes have become a popular method for connecting the physical and digital worlds. They are two-dimensional barcodes which look like a square full of smaller squares with oddly defined corners. They can be printed anywhere (on marketing literature, on walls) and can be scanned using a smartphone or tablet camera, directing users to online content such as websites, social media profiles, promotional offers, or booking platforms. QR codes cost literally zero to implement.

In the UK and Europe, 86% of smartphone users had scanned a QR Code at least once in their lifetime. 36.40 % scan at least one QR Code a week.

HTTPS://WWW.LXAHUB.COM/STORIES/QR-CODE-STATS-TRENDS

For aesthetics professionals, QR codes can be used to:

- **Enhance customer knowledge:** Put QR codes on printed marketing materials like brochures, posters, and flyers, as well as on in-office signage and product packaging, to provide easy access to digital resources like treatment information, before-and-after galleries or patient testimonials.
- **Streamline booking and follow-up processes:** Use QR codes to direct clients to online booking platforms, making it easier for them

to schedule appointments or consultations. Additionally, QR codes can be used on post-treatment materials to link to aftercare instructions, follow-up appointment scheduling, or feedback forms.

- **Track marketing performance:** QR codes can be embedded with unique tracking parameters, allowing you to monitor the effectiveness of different marketing materials and campaigns by analysing scan data and subsequent user behaviour.

Augmented Reality (AR)

Augmented Reality (AR) is a technology which overlays digital information, such as images, videos, or text, onto the user's view of the real world. It has become increasingly popular for marketing purposes, as it enables businesses to create engaging, interactive experiences that bridge the gap between digital and physical environments. The drawback is that very few environments currently support AR – it is usually made available through virtual reality (VR) headsets, and few people are using those yet. Even fewer are using them outside the home.

Even so, AR and VR are definitely coming. If you don't intend to use it yourself (designing AR/VR is expensive), you can expect big brands in aesthetics to develop AR applications and experiences. For aesthetics professionals, AR – or simulations of it – can be used to:

- **Showcase treatment results:** Allow clients to virtually "try on" different treatments, giving them a realistic preview of potential outcomes. This can be particularly useful for procedures such as injectables, skin rejuvenation, or body contouring.
- **Enhance in-office experiences:** Implement AR elements within your practice, such as interactive displays or virtual product demonstrations, to engage and educate clients during their visit.

Near Field Communication (NFC)

Near Field Communication (NFC) is a wireless communication technology that enables the transfer of data between two devices in close proximity. It is used particularly to facilitate contactless transactions, manage access security, share information, or trigger actions on a user's device. If you've ever paid for something by tapping your phone, you've used NFC – and that's a good example: it's called "Near Field" because it's highly localised, operating across only a few centimetres. NFC is also surprisingly cheap – it's not a marketing miracle, but it's a very economical way to execute a highly creative marketing campaign that brings the digital and physical together.

For aesthetics professionals, we can expect NFC applications to:

- **Streamline client interactions:** Embed NFC tags into marketing materials, business cards, or product packaging to quickly share information, direct clients to your website, or initiate a phone call or email.
- **Enhance the practice experience:** Use NFC technology to create interactive displays within your practice, allowing clients to access digital content by tapping their smartphones against a designated area.
- **Boost client loyalty:** Implement an NFC-enabled loyalty program, offering clients rewards or incentives for repeat visits. By storing loyalty information digitally, clients can easily track their progress and redeem rewards using their smartphone.

Geofencing

Finally, let's look at geofencing. Geofencing is a location-based marketing technique that uses GPS or radio frequency identification (RFID) technology to create virtual boundaries around a specific geographic area. When a user enters or exits the geofenced area, this can trigger a digital event

– they can, for example, receive targeted messages, promotions, or notifications on their devices.

For an aesthetics practice, geofencing can be used to:

- **Drive foot traffic:** Set up geofences around your practice or nearby high-traffic areas, such as shopping centres, to send targeted promotions and incentives to potential clients when they arrive in the vicinity. This can help capture the attention of nearby users and encourage them to visit your practice.
- **Enhance the customer experience:** Implement geofencing technology within your practice to trigger personalized welcome messages when clients arrive for their appointments. This can help create a seamless, tailored and delightful experience for each client.

Geofencing is technologically easy but does require authority from the customer – this may be obtained at the same time as other marketing permissions. It may also be embedded into an app and its permissions if you have one.

You're unlikely to use all of these techniques but you can see the point: QR codes, Augmented Reality (AR), Near Field Communication (NFC), and geofencing all offer powerful ways to integrate digital and physical marketing in sync into the aesthetics retail experience. By thoughtfully implementing these technologies, you can create immersive experiences that enhance the client journey, streamline interactions and even drive increased foot traffic, contributing to the bottom line.

ONE BRAND, EVERY CHANNEL

Integrating the digital and physical aspects of marketing for aesthetics professionals is all about creating a cohesive brand experience. That consistency across channels means you can give your customers a seamless experience that reinforces your brand identity, builds trust, and encourages those clients to engage with your practice both online and offline. Here are the basics:

- **Establish a consistent visual identity:** Your visual identity, which includes your logo, colour palette, typography and imagery, should be consistent across all marketing materials, both online and offline. This helps to create a strong, recognizable brand that clients can easily identify and associate with your practice. Apply your visual identity consistently on your website, social media profiles, email marketing, print materials, in-office signage, and any other touchpoints clients may encounter.

- **Align your messaging:** Your messaging should be consistent across all channels too, reinforcing your unique selling points and highlighting the benefits of your treatments and services. This includes your brand voice and tone, which should reflect the personality and values of your practice. Maybe you're professional and informative; maybe more casual and friendly. Maybe you target male professionals; or 'Yummy Mummies'. Either way, maintain a consistent voice in your written content.

- **Create seamless transitions between channels:** To create a cohesive experience, make it easy for clients to move between your digital and physical marketing channels. For example, if you're promoting a special offer through email marketing, make sure your website provides clear instructions on how to find your practice, book appointments, and access any relevant information about the offer; and then, when they arrive at the practice, the experience is similarly smooth and brand-consistent.

- **Personalize the client experience:** Use digital tools to personalize the client experience, both online and offline. By collecting and analyzing data on client preferences, behaviours, and interactions, you can create customized marketing messages, offers, and in-store experiences that cater to each client's unique needs and desires. This level of personalization will help you to build strong client relationships, encouraging loyalty and repeat business.

- **Train your staff:** Got a team? They play a critical role in creating a cohesive brand experience, as they are the face of your practice and the main point of contact for clients. If you've ever been to Mcdonald's and wondered how the same experience endures around the globe, it's because every member of staff is singing from the same hymn sheet. To some degree, that's incredibly boring, but your staff should certainly be well-trained and knowledgeable enough to confidently guide clients through the process of interacting with QR codes, NFC technology and AR experiences as well as marketing collateral and printouts. Your staff should also be aligned with your brand's messaging, visual identity, and overall mission, so they can effectively communicate with clients during every in-person interaction.

"Customers will never love a company until the employees love it first."

GUY KAWASAKI, AUTHOR OF 'RICH DAD, POOR DAD'

All of these are good practices in any event and should be part of your efforts to provide an excellent customer experience. However, as we move to an increasingly hybrid world where digital and physical marketing tools rub up against digital and physical experiences of the provision of services, it's ever more important – both from the point of view of preserving cash and also of being effective – to present one brand and one experience, no matter what tech you deploy.

CHECKLIST

☑ Ensure a consistent brand experience across all channels, both digital and physical.

☑ Use tools like QR codes, Augmented Reality (AR), Near Field Communication (NFC), and geofencing not as gimmicks but to bridge the digital-physical gap in marketing.

☑ Create seamless transitions between channels for clients, making it easy to move between digital and physical touchpoints.

☑ Personalize the client experience whenever you can.

☑ Train your staff to be knowledgeable about new technologies and aligned with your brand's messaging, visual identity, and mission.

LEGAL AND ETHICAL STANDARDS IN AESTHETICS MARKETING

There's a shorter summary of some of the legal requirements for marketers in Chapter 6, "Email Marketing", but both marketing and aesthetics are such minefields of legal complexity that I thought it might be worth examining the key themes at work.

LEGAL FRAMEWORKS

Let's start with data privacy. The General Data Protection Regulation (GDPR) came into force in May 2018. This European regulation (it still stands despite Britain's decision to leave the EU, and the UK will implement something similar to GDPR in good time) aims to protect the privacy and personal data of citizens, and it has a direct impact on your digital marketing activities. To comply with the GDPR, you need to consider:

- **Consent:** When collecting personal data (name, email address, phone number, etc.) from clients, you must obtain their explicit consent. This means using clear and concise language, and ensuring that the consent is freely given, specific, informed, and unambiguous.
- **Data minimisation:** Collect only the data that is necessary for your marketing activities, and do not store it for longer than necessary.

- **Data access and portability:** Your clients have the right to access, correct and delete their personal data. They also have the right to data portability, which means they can obtain and reuse their data across different services.
- **Security:** Implement all appropriate security measures to protect personal data from unauthorized access, disclosure, alteration, or destruction.

GDPR applies to data usage and storage. Another set of regulations, The Privacy and Electronic Communications Regulations (PECR), enforces best practice for marketing. The PECR is a UK-specific regulation that governs electronic communications, including email, SMS, and telemarketing. To stay compliant with the PECR, follow these guidelines:

- **Opt-in consent:** As with GDPR, always obtain opt-in consent before sending electronic marketing messages to clients. This means that they must actively agree to receive marketing communications from you. Pre-ticked boxes or implied consent are not acceptable.
- **Opt-out mechanism:** You must include an easy-to-use and clear opt-out mechanism in all your electronic marketing communications. This allows clients to unsubscribe from your marketing messages at any time, even though they have opted in beforehand.
- **Identifying the sender:** You must clearly identify your aesthetics practice as the sender of the marketing communication and provide a valid contact address.
- **Cookie compliance:** If your website uses cookies or other tracking technologies, you must obtain the user's consent and provide clear information about their use and purpose.

"Marketers not only have to think about what is profitable, but also what is right. The best marketing is ethical marketing."

PROF. PHILIP KOTLER

In Chapter 10, we look at Influencer Marketing. I can honestly say that whilst advertising is well regulated in the UK, by both The Advertising Standards Authority (ASA) and the Committee of Advertising Practice (CAP), like all regulators, they are slow to respond to new uses of media. Influencer marketing and advertising in Virtual Reality, for example, are still barely regulated. You can expect the law to catch up as it always does, and I expect regulation to develop significantly in these areas.

However, the ASA does have some teeth. It's the UK's independent regulator for advertising across all media, including digital marketing. CAP, meanwhile, is responsible for writing and maintaining the UK Advertising Codes, which provide guidelines for advertisers to follow. To ensure your digital marketing activities comply with the ASA and CAP, keep the following principles in mind:

- **Legal, decent, honest, and truthful:** Your communications must be legal, decent, honest, and truthful. This means avoiding false claims or misleading information about your services, qualifications, or the benefits of your treatments. The aesthetics business is very much under the microscope in this context, so please stick to the truth!
- **Substantiation:** You must be able to substantiate any claims you make in your marketing materials with appropriate evidence. For example, if you claim that a particular treatment is effective in reducing wrinkles, you should have clinical studies or other credible evidence to support that fact.
- **Social responsibility:** Marketing communications must be prepared with a sense of responsibility to consumers and society. This means avoiding promoting unhealthy body images or pressuring clients into undergoing treatments they may not need.
- **Targeting:** Be mindful of the audience you are targeting with your marketing communications. Do not target vulnerable groups or those who may be easily influenced by your marketing messages. Additionally, avoid marketing to children, unless your services are

specifically aimed at them and can demonstrably bring them a benefit without sacrificing safety or legality. In the online world where there is no such thing as the "9 pm watershed", and where on social media it is all too easy for children to sign up for services, it is harder than ever to observe an ethical approach to targeting.

The Consumer Rights Act 2015 consolidates consumer protection laws and aims to ensure that consumers receive clear and accurate information about the goods and services that they consume. Marketing isn't specifically the theme of this legislation (there's plenty more to the Act than we're looking at here), but it does have an impact on the way you communicate. As an aesthetics practice, it is important to comply with the Consumer Rights Act with:

- **Accurate and clear information:** Provide accurate and clear information about your treatments, prices, and any additional costs (such as consultation fees). This should include information about the qualifications and experience of the practitioners who will perform any treatments.
- **No hidden fees or charges:** Be transparent about all costs and fees, and do not add hidden charges to your clients' bills. Ensure that your clients are aware of any cancellation or late fees they may incur.

You may – should, in fact – also be a member of a professional body, such as the British Association of Cosmetic Nurses (BACN), the British College of Aesthetic Medicine (BCAM), or the Joint Council for Cosmetic Practitioners (JCCP). Each of these organisations has its own code of conduct, which members are expected to follow. Familiarise yourself with the relevant code of conduct and adhere to its guidelines in your marketing activities.

ETHICS IN AESTHETICS

In addition to complying with the legal requirements outlined above, it is crucial for aesthetics practices to consider the ethical implications of their marketing activities.

The law doesn't say that you need to be ethical. You can be a dismal mercenary and still not break the law. But you'll do a lot better by being aligned with the values and expectations of your clients and society at large – including in the marketing claims you make.

Today's customer really wants to get their services – including aesthetics – from someone they trust and who cares about the same things that they do. Here are a few things to consider...

Transparency and Honesty: Being transparent and honest in your marketing communications will help you build trust with your clients. It'll keep you on the right side of the law and ultimately develop your brand, too. This means providing accurate information about your treatments and pricing, as well as the qualifications of your practitioners. Avoid exaggerating the benefits of a treatment or using misleading language.

- Clearly describe the risks and potential side effects of treatments in your marketing materials and during consultations.
- Don't use before-and-after photos that are manipulated or not representative of typical results.
- Be open about any affiliations or partnerships with manufacturers or other entities that may influence your recommendations.

Promote Realistic Expectations: It is vital to promote realistic expectations for the results of treatments. Overpromising or making exaggerated claims about the outcomes of a procedure will lead to client dissatisfaction and harm your reputation.

■ Use language that reflects the variable nature of treatment outcomes. For example, instead of saying a treatment "will" produce a certain result, use phrases like "may help" or "can contribute to."

■ During consultations, discuss the individual factors that can influence treatment outcomes, such as age, skin type, and lifestyle habits.

■ Encourage clients to view their treatment as part of a holistic approach to self-care rather than a quick fix.

Respect Client Autonomy: This means acknowledging every client's right to make informed decisions about their treatment. Your marketing materials and consultations should empower clients to make choices based on accurate information without feeling pressured or manipulated.

■ Never use high-pressure sales tactics, such as limited-time offers, discounts that encourage impulsive decision-making or forcing clients into a decision.

■ Offer comprehensive consultations that allow clients to ask questions and voice their concerns before committing to a treatment.

■ Encourage a culture in your practice that values client autonomy and discourages aggressive sales techniques.

Body Positivity and Inclusivity: Your marketing communications should promote a positive and inclusive view of beauty, rather than perpetuating harmful stereotypes or body-shaming. As an industry, we need to be the source of a healthy relationship between our clients and their bodies.

■ Use diverse and representative images of clients in your marketing materials, reflecting a range of ages, body types, and ethnicities.

■ Avoid language that stigmatizes or shames certain physical features, such as "fixing" or "correcting" perceived flaws.

■ Encourage clients to focus on their overall well-being and self-confidence, rather than solely on physical appearance.

Environmental and Social Responsibility: Lastly, consider the environmental and social impact of your marketing activities and the products and services you offer. Demonstrating a commitment to sustainability and social responsibility will help to attract clients who share these values, but they should be second nature to you anyway.

- Choose eco-friendly marketing materials, such as recycled paper or digital advertising options that reduce waste.
- Implement sustainable practices in your clinic, such as energy-efficient lighting and recycling programs.
- Select products and suppliers that prioritize ethical sourcing, fair labour practices, and minimal environmental impact.
- Educate your clients about the environmental and social impact of the treatments and products you offer and provide guidance on how they can make more sustainable choices.

Remember, ethical marketing is not just about ticking boxes or avoiding negative publicity – it is an opportunity to demonstrate your values, create meaningful connections, and make a positive impact on the world around you. In the long run, investing in ethical marketing practices leads to greater client loyalty, increased referrals, and a more sustainable and successful business.

CHECKLIST

☑ Review the key principles of GDPR and PECR to ensure data privacy compliance.

☑ Keep your marketing communications legal, decent, honest, and truthful.

☑ Encourage body positivity: avoid language that stigmatises or shames.

☑ Operate in an environmentally and socially responsible way in your clinic and marketing.

NEED HELP?
GET AN AGENCY

If you've read this book from cover to cover, you'll know that a strong digital presence is essential for success and that marketing is, well, complicated. You could spend all day just on one technique. That's why many aesthetics practice managers decide to partner with a digital marketing agency to help them reach their audiences and generate more leads.

PICK YOUR PERFECT PARTNER

Picking the right agency can be a daunting task, but a well-informed decision will lead to long-term benefits for your practice and possibly even transformative degrees of success. In this chapter, we will discuss the key factors to consider when choosing a digital marketing agency.

But before you begin your search, decide on the parameters. You need to have a clear understanding of your practice's marketing objectives, or you won't know what to ask for (sure, it should be a partnership and your agency should be able to advise, but it's entirely reasonable to have a ballpark in mind). Here are the questions to ask yourself before picking up the phone or browsing:

- **What are your marketing goals?** Are you looking to raise brand awareness, generate leads, or increase conversions? "Everything" is a perfectly reasonable answer.

- **What marketing services do you require?** For example, do you need help with website design, search engine optimization (SEO), pay-per-click (PPC) advertising, or social media management? You can probably do some of these. Some you may actually enjoy. Others will fill you with dread. Or you may just want someone to take the whole thing off your back (us agencies prefer this, too – not because it's more profitable, but because we can be holistic in the way we operate).
- **What is your marketing budget?** Having a clear budget will help you select an agency that can provide the services you want within your financial constraints. That doesn't mean you need to admit your budget upfront. There may be some negotiation. But agencies don't want tyre-kickers, and you don't want either a Rolls Royce or a Robin Reliant when something in the middle is right up your street.

Once you have a clear understanding of your marketing needs, research potential digital marketing agencies until you get to a shortlist of 2-5 options.

- **Get recommendations** from colleagues in the aesthetics industry or other business owners. The vast majority of work in my own agency comes from recommendations. We prefer it, and clients do, too.
- **Conduct online searches** using relevant keywords, such as "digital marketing agency for aesthetics practices" or "digital marketing agency UK."
- **Browse industry forums** or social media groups to find agencies that have been mentioned or recommended by others.

As you research, take note of each agency's core services, industry experience, and client portfolio. This will help you narrow down your options and identify the agencies that are most likely to meet your needs.

Check their past work and success stories. This will give you an insight into their creative style, technical expertise, and ability to deliver results.

Plenty of agencies will be really good, but just won't have your style or ethos at heart. Only a good look at their past work will give you this gut feel, and you would be well advised to follow it. A portfolio should give you comfort in:

- **Relevant experience in the aesthetics industry:** An agency with a track record of success in your industry will have a deeper understanding of your target audience, the unique challenges you face and the needs of the end consumer.
- **Diverse range of services:** Ensure the agency has experience with the specific marketing services you require, such as SEO, PPC, social, etc.
- **Proven results:** Look for quantifiable results, such as increases in website traffic, leads, or conversions, etc.
- **Client testimonials:** Positive feedback from clients will give you confidence in the agency's work style, communication, and overall satisfaction.

Once you have narrowed down your options, schedule an initial work-through with each of your top choices. During the consultation, discuss your marketing needs, goals, and budget. Use this opportunity to ask questions and assess the agency's expertise, creativity, and understanding of your industry.

Here are some questions to ask:

- How do you approach digital marketing for aesthetics practices? What strategies have you found to be most effective?
- How do you stay up-to-date with industry trends and best practice?
- Can you provide examples of successful campaigns you have executed for other aesthetics practices?
- How do you measure the success of your campaigns, and what reporting tools do you use to track progress and results?
- What is your pricing structure, and how does it align with our budget?

- How do you communicate with clients? What can we expect in terms of regular updates and meetings?
- Do you offer any guarantees or assurances related to your services or results?
- How does your team stay up-to-date with regulatory requirements, such as GDPR and other data protection laws, relevant to the aesthetics industry in the UK?

Equally, keep your ears open for the questions they ask you. Are they genuinely interested in you as a client? Are they invested in your success? As an agency owner myself, I'm interested in clients who we can grow with – not a transactional relationship which only benefits one or other side of the coin. A successful partnership with a digital marketing agency goes beyond their technical expertise and proven results; it's about two businesses working and growing together. That's why it's also essential to understand the agency's culture and team dynamics. After all, everyone can work together in the good times, but when the chips are down and you need help with a crisis at 2 am, will these folks be at the end of the phone line? Ask some of these questions in your assessment:

- **Core values:** Does the agency share similar values to your practice, such as a commitment to innovation, quality, or customer service?
- **Team structure:** What is the agency's team structure, and how will they assign resources to your account? Ideally, you want a dedicated account manager and a team of specialists in the specific marketing services you require. You don't want the MD on day one but just an intern by day 5!
- **Communication style:** Do they listen to your needs and respond thoughtfully, or do they seem more focused on selling?
- **Collaboration:** How does the agency approach collaboration with clients? Look for an agency that values your input and is open to incorporating your ideas and feedback into their strategies.

On the basis of these considerations, who gives you good vibes, and who just isn't making you feel excited about working together? We consistently find that after a meeting, any considerations about price tend to fade away – it's all about partnership, collaboration and a commitment to taking the business somewhere new.

And that's because a successful digital marketing strategy is rarely a one-off project; it requires ongoing optimization, adaptation, and growth. It's important to choose an agency that can support your practice's evolving needs over time. Can the agency accommodate your practice's growth and changing needs? For example, if you expand your service offerings or target new markets, can the agency adapt its strategies accordingly? Does the agency offer ongoing support and maintenance for services like website updates, SEO optimization, and PPC campaign management? And how does the agency stay current with industry trends, best practice, and emerging technologies? A forward-thinking agency will be committed to helping you stay ahead of the competition.

It's an ongoing, collaborative process, so take the time to find an agency that aligns with your practice's needs, values and objectives and will work with you to navigate the complexities of the digital world and grow your business.

I would, of course, invite you to consider my agency, LTF Digital.

LTF is the trusted name for all things digital in the medical aesthetics market. We partner with aesthetics clinic owners, pharma companies and manufacturers in the UK, US, Australia, New Zealand, Dubai and Canada.

You can find us at:

E: us@ltf.email
T: 01327 828 443
W: https://ltf.digital/

CHECKLIST

☑ Start by defining your marketing goals and the services you think you'll need.

☑ Establish a budget to help you find an agency that can offer the services you need within your financial constraints.

☑ Gather recommendations from colleagues and industry contacts – recommendations are golden.

☑ Research and then create a shortlist.

☑ Look for relevant industry experience, a diverse range of services and proven results.

☑ Assess agency culture and team dynamics – you want a partner for the long haul.

DISCOVER THE MERZ DIGITAL ACADEMY

Marketing isn't easy – mainly because it's a full-time job. I've built a whole career around it, and I don't get many days off! However, there is plenty of help at hand. I still think that even the smallest practice can benefit from the assistance of an agency, but before you make that leap, you can make a start with the Merz Aesthetics Digital Academy.

Merz Aesthetics is, of course, a global leader in aesthetics, with the Ultherapy® and Belotero® brands in their stable, among others. I have worked with them for the past two years to create a completely free Digital Academy designed to help aesthetics entrepreneurs to take their digital marketing to another level.

It's a comprehensive three-month programme designed to upskill HCPs in their own digital marketing and improve the growth of your clinic as a result. The programme is a combination of online learning, live coaching, comprehensive assessment tools, and step-by-step action plans, all delivered by a team of dedicated digital coaches, six of them with a combined 70 years of experience in digital marketing, most of which has been gained in the medical aesthetics market. The Academy covers all the areas we've looked at in this book (SEO, Web Design, Automation, Social Media and more).

And perhaps even more importantly, it's structured to give you insights from simple data points: how effective your marketing is now, where you need to be, where the gaps are, and therefore, where you should put your marketing effort and budget in order to get the most effective results. In a world where all marketing costs money and business is intensely competitive, the Academy isn't just full of good advice; it'll set you off in the right strategic direction.

Feedback on The Digital Academy has been fantastic (you can see what some of our alumni are saying, below) and we're seeing tangible results including significant increases in Google presence, search views, traffic to practitioners' websites, and most importantly, an upsurge in patient bookings directly attributable to the actions and tools put in place by the programme.

"Very happy with the results; I now have a consistent stream of new clients who find me effortlessly through my website and social media channels. The clients who make enquiries or book in with me are ready to act on their goals, and are willing to listen, as well as trust in my expertise. I'm scaling up my clinic!"

TD AESTHETICS

"Such a useful program, my client engagement has really improved as a result. I had got lazy after initially setting everything up several years ago, so this gave me the impetus to update my digital presence."

TALLENT MEDICAL

"The Merz Aesthetics Digital Academy has been a rewarding experience. My digital coach guided me through gaps in my marketing and gave me a detailed action plan to increase my patient numbers and increase my presence on Google, my business and the web. I am so thankful for their expertise and continue to see growth in my business."

ASPIRE AESTHETICS

As clinicians, we can manage all the clinical aspects well, but the business can be a little more challenging, in particular, marketing online. Being involved with Mertz and the touch field, collaboration has been fantastic; we've been guided to optimize our business and our clinic to grow in positive ways, and we have noticed some significant gains in interest in our clinic, our Google ranking and how we can best invest our time in the right platforms. So all in all, it's been a fantastic journey.

RKV AESTHETICS

To find out more, speak to your Merz Aesthetics Representative.

Milton Keynes UK
Ingram Content Group UK Ltd.
UKHW052058130823
426801UK00002B/2/J

9 781805 412854